HOW TO GET
AND HOLD
KEY ACCOUNTS

L. H. Clark

HOW TO GET
AND HOLD
KEY ACCOUNTS

The Complete Guide for the Manufacturer's Rep

McGRAW-HILL BOOK COMPANY

New York   St. Louis   San Francisco   Auckland   Düsseldorf
Johannesburg   Kuala Lumpur   London   Mexico   Montreal   New Delhi
Panama   Paris   São Paulo   Singapore   Sydney   Tokyo   Toronto

55679

Library of Congress Cataloging in Publication Data

Clark, LH, date.
How to get and hold key accounts.

1. Manufacturers' agents. I. Title.
HF5422.C55   658.85   75-9560
ISBN 0-07-011160-X

1 2 3 4 5 6 7 8 9 0 BPBP 7 8 4 3 2 1 0 9 8 7 6 5

The editors for this book were W. Hodson Mogan and Carolyn Nagy, the designer was Elliot Epstein, and the production supervisor was George Oechsner. It was set in Baskerville by University Graphics, Inc.

It was printed and bound by The Book Press.

For Two Priscillas

CONTENTS

CHAPTER TWO.

Your Relations with Your Key Accounts

WHO CAN USE THIS BOOK PROFITABLY?

This is not a book for aspiring sales novices.

This book is for reps who have been through the mill. These reps know that success in selling is not only a matter of being familiar with the product. It's also a matter of understanding and handling yourself in a way that inspires the respect and confidence of the people with whom you do business.

They know that profitability means selling key accounts and keeping them sold . . . that good fellowship is involved in selling as it is in every human activity. They also know when to shut up.

They have discovered that customer golf is not the be-all and end-all of handling key accounts.

They know that service is seven-tenths of key account holding.

No one has to tell them that a sale is not complete until there is a reorder, either "as had" or in larger volume.

They want more profit.

They want money and status, because status without money is an empty success. They have found that money usually creates its own prestige.

A great number of these successful sales veterans have decided to become manufacturers' representatives in order to capitalize on a native sales ability which has been honed fine by experience. Most of this book is related to their problems.

Some readers have decided to stay with a company because

they see a good chance to rise both in pay and in position. Part of this book relates to their problems. Then there are people who have been looking at their bankbooks and wondering whether to stay where they are or become reps. This book will point out some of the obstacles and disadvantages and how to overcome them.

Senior salesreps have the same problems whether they are in business for themselves or are account executives with large companies. They usually do not work "by the book." In fact, many of them are continually rewriting the book. That is why they can learn from each other.

Many corporate people, who are also rewriting the book, will be dealing with manufacturers' reps. This is a good way to discover their problems and their attitudes.

Every part of this book relates to specific problems and how they have been answered in today's market.

There are numerous blank spaces left so that you can make notations, because no two reps sell the same way successfully. The blank spaces will enable you to note your own probable directions.

All the questions and answers, all the tips, all the letters, and all the experiences have only one goal: *profitability*. That is the real name of the game. Everything else is a side issue.

Ultimate success today comes to the rep who can sell and keep key accounts. That is why everything in this book points to getting and holding key accounts.

Key accounts represent the zenith of your profitability to yourself and to your associates.

Profitability is the key to a full existence.

ACKNOWLEDGMENTS

First of all, I want to acknowledge my gratitude to every account who ever bought anything from me—and my debt to every account who never did. From both of them I learned the essentials of my profession—selling.

One man who stands out as an inspiration, both as a spur and as one who encouraged, is Mr. Philip H. Perry. From him I learned the value of building from a sure foundation of knowledge . . . that sales are really repeat orders . . . and that a clearly written letter, timed correctly, can work wonders.

HOW TO GET
AND HOLD
KEY ACCOUNTS

CHAPTER ONE

Pointers to profitability

KEY ACCOUNTS—WHO ARE THEY? WHY GO AFTER THEM?

A key account is any customer who can use up to 100 percent of your capacity if you are a small business. If you are a medium size business, a key account has a potential volume of 25 percent of your capacity.

If General Motors can only use ½ of 1 percent of your production, then General Motors, for all its size, is *not* a key account. But H. & R. Blow, Inc., which does $12 million a year, pays on time, and uses 25 percent of your capacity, is a key account.

Usually key accounts are large, well-known targets whom everyone goes after for two reasons: volume and on-time payment. Key accounts usually discount their bills. They demand the best service possible; they are willing to pay for it—and they get it!

You can't just walk in off the street and ask a key-account buyer for a chance because you need the commissions. Everyone else does, too.

Just why should the buyer give you a chance to quote? Why should he or she need you? You have to plan your strategy to make them need you. Can you come up with an idea or a product which will save their company money? Time? Can you suggest new production values? Will dealing with you tend to enhance the buyer's image with top management?

A key account demands research. You have to know its needs intimately. You have to become so well psyched into its business that you know when production is going to call for your products before the buyer does.

You have to know which principal is going to fit a key account's needs. And if you don't have any principals who fit the description, you'll go out and get them.

If it takes all this trouble, worry, and bother to get a key account and, even worse, to hold on to it, why do it? Why not go after the "easy stuff"—whatever that is?

Because when you get and hold a key account, you are made.

It's as simple as that.

Your income begins to rise immediately. If the key account (or key accounts) is big enough, it can rise indefinitely.

Because you handle key accounts, the president will come out front to greet you personally when you visit the plant.

You are a V.I.P.

Your requests for estimates and samples rate special handling. Why? "C. W. handles the big ones" is enough reason.

The plant will do things for you they wouldn't think of doing for their "ordinary" reps; you are one of *the* reps—one of our "key people." You represent business that is the lifeblood of the profit and loss columns. Without the business you represent they'd have to shut down a shift; their overhead would start to rise.

It's unfair. We know that everyone should be treated the same way. But reps who can get and hold key accounts are treated better—lots better.

Benefits from handling key accounts are reflected in the rest of your business, too—not only because the factories give you preferential treatment, but because your self-confidence grows. You find you are able to make sales no one else ever could . . . and at good prices, too.

Confidence enables you to handle everything better.

All this because you can get and keep key accounts.
That makes you tops in your field.
That's why key-account sales are every rep's goal in life.

PROFITABILITY IN POLICY MAKING

Surveying the Field

1. Will you concentrate on one field?

   a. Is your territory concentrated enough to allow you to call on only one type of account?

   b. Is your product line wide enough to give you concentrated scope so that you can do well in a geographically small territory?

POINT. One of your most heartbreaking decisions will be to turn down an obviously good and profitable product because you can't handle it with justification to yourself. If you do take it on, you'll be handling two separate lines at 50 percent efficiency, running twice as hard to make half as much. This is when you have to put on sunglasses to keep the gold out of your eyes.

2. The smaller and more concentrated your territory, the better its potential profitability because:

   a. You do less traveling.

   b. You can give your accounts and principals better service.

   c. The overhead is lower in both travel costs and telephone bills, the only two variables in your overhead.

Your territory is most likely set up already because of either prior commitments or natural boundaries. Figure how you are going to concentrate to get the most out of it. Don't let your thinking be overcome by geography; a larger territory does not mean automatically larger profits.

Set a goal for yourself of $250,000 before you hire anyone. Can the territory stand sales of $500,000 yearly after five years?

Concentration and low overhead should be the goals of your sales policy. Why lose all your hard-earned commissions to careless thinking?

Be Profitable to Yourself

When a former company account executive goes independent, one thought should be kept in mind all the time: "I am in business for myself." The emphasis, at all times, is on the word *business.*

You make money only when you are profitable to others— while being profitable to yourself.

There is no other way.

When principals are allowed to run your business, you will soon end up broke as well as disillusioned.

Therefore your decisions must be profitable to your accounts and to you.

"Let 'em all in on it" is a fine idea as long as you—and your accounts—are in on it, too.

WHO GETS TO BE A SUCCESSFUL MANUFACTURER'S REPRESENTATIVE?

The Hundred-to-One Shot

If you have never sold before and have no accounts who know you, ninety-nine times out of a hundred, *don't do it!*

The hundredth chance is someone offering you a line which is already established, which you do not have to pioneer at all, and which will bring in immediate income.

Unless you are a relative, you are usually offered this opportunity only because you have some skill: engineering, accounting, fashion, pharmaceutical, etc.—knowledge which is temporarily deemed more necessary than sales skills.

If you become a manufacturer's rep under these conditions,

get yourself a sales manual and study hard. Learn how to sell as quickly as you can. The conditions under which you were given the line are soon going to change, and you will find the need for sales skills paramount if you are going to survive.

The Big-Company Account Executive

You are an account executive for a large, well-known company. You have done a good job but, for some reason you'll never discover, you have not gone ahead with your age group. You know now that you'll never advance more than a step or two. You know there are better things inside you than the company has seen. That is what is impelling you to take the ultimate step and go into business for yourself as a rep.

You have sold a line to a group of well-rated accounts in one territory, and you have done well. You know that territory better than your own backyard.

The disadvantage: the product you sold is one which is manufactured by large companies which have their own sales staffs. Therefore the chance of your getting to represent something like it which can be guaranteed under all conditions is practically nil.

Your advantage: you know the accounts and they know and trust you. This is your most important asset, capital, raison d'être, or whatever.

How do you figure it out?

Get a list of your accounts together and figure out what they use in common—what they *need* in common. Not the high-priced, bought-once-every-five-years, title A materials—nothing for which board of directors' approval is needed. It takes years to get into a position where you can sell these items comfortably.

In starting out, you need nonglamorous products: products which are bought every week, disposable items, small tools, anything which a plant or company needs all the time.

These are the bread-and-butter items which lead to selling the high-priced, high-commission, glamour products. With fast-moving products from good sources, you establish yourself with your accounts as a dependable supplier.

You also start getting an income more quickly.

Income (as no one has to tell you) is the best morale builder in the world.

The Employee of a Small or Medium-sized Outfit

You have been working for a small or medium-sized firm which is becoming heir-conditioned. Or it is about to be taken over by a company "which is here to bring skilled modern management to the company. We want every one of you to be here ten years from now—if you can fit in with our philosophy!" You soon realize it is only a question of time before you will have to move or start your own business.

You don't have the capital to start a business like the one you are in now. You do have enough to keep you going for a year or, certainly, you know how to get it!

You decide to become a representative because you know your customers and what they need.

Again the fastest way to an **income** is to sell volume products to companies that know you.

Fast-moving, volume products are the most competitive. Quotes will go to five or six people. You'll lose more than you'll get, in the beginning. But the more quotes you get, the more orders you'll get, too. The more quotes, the wider your business acquaintance becomes as well.

Any purposeful sales activity is better than the frustration of waiting around for that one big quote which will make you rich:

1. *If* you get the request for quotation. ("Hell, you want to give this to a new rep? How d'you know they can deliver?")

2. *If* you get the right price. ("They're new reps. We better put a lot of safety into this estimate.")

3. *If* the project isn't canceled after you've worked on it for a year. ("Our economist's latest projections have persuaded the Board of Directors to defer. . . .")

4. *If* you can wait around for two or three years for your commission. ("We only pay upon turnkey delivery.")

Big orders—and big commissions—are the beautiful icing in the rep business.

It's the steady income from numerous small orders which makes them possible.

CAN *YOU* PROFITABLY START A MANUFACTURER'S REP BUSINESS?

Only you know.

Only you can fool yourself.

Some reps should not be in business for themselves. They are high on sales ability but deficient in the profit instinct that makes a business survive.

Other salesreps can fulfill themselves only in directing their own destinies.

Here's a checklist:

1. Do you have the expertise necessary in your chosen field?

   a. When you are on your own, you have got to know what you are talking about. You'll have no one to cross-fertilize with. No one will correct errors which will now cost *you* money. Your principals are only (and rightly) interested in their own problems. Your accounts expect *you* to be the problem solver.

   b. In connection with this, don't be shunted into another field just because it looks like a winner from a distance. This happens more often than not and is a killer to new rep businesses—and to old ones, too.

      If you don't know the field you are going into and are taking on a strange product line, you have two pioneering jobs to do. That's too many at one time.

2. Do you have the self-discipline that will get you out in the

early morning, to figure out closely scheduled sales interviews, and to work like a dog until you get home—when more work will commence?

Will you have the self-discipline to miss favorite TV shows, football games, and card parties because you have to get out paperwork, orders, requests for quotations, and information from your customers to your principals, check on shipments, figure commission statements, etc.— all the million and one things you have to do when you're in business for yourself by yourself?

Are you ready to do this for four years? That's how long it will take you to get near the real money.

If you are ulcer material, being a rep will really bring it out.

You need a concerned, tough matter-of-factness to stand the pressure.

If you still feel you can make it, read on:

3. Do you have a year's living expenses in the bank?

    a. If you go into business with at least two good principals, you should be meeting expenses within a year. It takes three years for accounts you've never called upon to consider you established. It takes four years to come into the big volume that makes the whole thing worthwhile.

    b. Key accounts are your goal. They can make it happen. If you've called upon them before, it takes about a year to change them over in volume. If you've never sold them, the remainder of this book is devoted to bringing down the time element from three years to eighteen months.

4. Will my friends in business help me?

    a. Only so far as helping you helps them. No one should expect any more. Discount all promises 75 percent. If you do better, it will be a pleasant surprise.

b. It is up to you when going into business to get principals who can offer something your business friends will be glad to buy. That is part of your expertise in the field.

5. Should I go in with a partner at once?

   a. Unless you know your partner's track record intimately and not from hearsay . . . *no*

   b. Unless your prospective partner is putting up an equal amount of money . . . *no*

   c. If you have both worked together before and know each other's strengths and weaknesses and you know that he is a terrific negotiator while your strength is in presentation
or

If you can handle money and he can't . . . or vice versa . . . in other words, if you complement each other . . . *yes*

Contrary to belief, it is not necessary to like a partner personally. You are not in business to form a social club. You are there to make a success.

It is absolutely necessary to have mutual respect.

Sounds tough?

It is.

The rewards are correspondingly high. They are self-respect, being someone in the business community, and financial success.

Most of all, it's being in complete charge of yourself.

HOW DO YOU GET YOUR FIRST PRINCIPAL?

To describe this in detail is as futile as telling a young man how to meet a girl. Everyone does it in his own fashion.

There are, however, certain guidelines.

1. There are salesreps who have gotten to know their fields remarkably well. They have become so well known that

principals—usually the competition—seek them out with offers.

2. Some reps begin as account executives for a large corporation in a fringe territory. The company (or its computer) decides there is not enough potential in the territory. However, they do not want to give up the investment they have made in it. They offer it to their territory salesrep on an independent basis. This is now a basic line.

3. There are reps who started their business life working for other reps. They have liked the hard challenge and comparative liberty of the life. Principals stake them to another territory.

But you are not one of these three. How do you go about getting your first principal?

You narrow down the territory you can cover profitably. You know that territory intimately. You have accounts there you are selling now.

Then you watch the ads in the *MANA Journal,* in *The New York Times,* and *The Wall Street Journal.* You keep a steady watch in your own metropolitan-area newspaper, and naturally you read all your business magazines.

You know of manufacturers who are not doing that well in your territory who put out a good product at a price.

You hear of a line which is being let go for a number of reasons, none of which looks fatal to you.

A buyer friend (and this is always one of the best sources) casually remarks that so and so is looking for a rep.

You stumble across an old competitor at a business show who needs someone in your territory.

In other words, you keep your eyes and ears open, put out feelers, and smell around for an opening.

After all, that is how you make sales. Getting a principal is like making another sale. Once you spot a quarry, you do your homework, come up with an idea that is profitable to both of you, and go after it.

SHOULD YOU INSIST ON A CONTRACT WITH PRINCIPALS?

There are some people in this world with whom you can do business on a handshake. They are very few and you have to know them personally, because they don't shake hands that often.

If good fences make good neighbors, then good contracts or letters of intent, properly carried out, make for the best relationship between rep and principal. When you have an agreement, there is no "But you promised me that adjacent territory within a year" or "We agreed that you would handle that certain account for 8 percent instead of 10 percent."

Think of it this way. Would you take a large order from an account without an order number to start with and a written order to follow?

Well, here you are about to barter away your most valuable commodity—**time**—without an agreement on how you are to be paid for it.

PARTNER OR EMPLOYEE—WHICH DO YOU NEED?

As in all really important matters, the answer to this one lies within yourself.

If you are asking this question because your income is too small or your territory isn't "right," forget it. In that case you can't afford an employee. And the only partner who will be interested is usually one who is suffering from financial exhaustion.

However, if you are beginning to find yourself overwhelmed with paperwork, of ir you find you can't make the calls you have to fast enough, then the question arises legitimately.

First, decide who you are.

If you are a lone wolf and don't like consultations, you'll need an employee. If you like to talk your problems over with "someone as smart as I am," you'll need a partner.

Don't mistake yourself for a lone wolf because you once admired Gary Cooper. Don't think you'll need a partner just because you happen to be courteous.

If it's to be a partner, no matter how well you know each other, even if you played on the same Little League team, have a regular contract signed between you.

It's a strange thing, but prosperity ruins more partnerships than adversity ever did. In other words, you'll both fight your way up side by side. It's when you get on top that the arguments begin. That's when rules which have been spelled out in advance can help a partnership survive.

If you have a written contract and you do break up, then at least most of your hard-earned money won't be going to the lawyers.

WOMEN IN BUSINESS: THEY WERE ALWAYS "HERE"

The tendency to treat women—either buyers or salesreps—as "special" is a highly unprofitable attitude. It does them no good; it does your business no good, either.

A buyer—man or woman—is not going to respond to sex, sweetness, and light if service and price are not forthcoming. When women buyers first came onto the scene, companies sent their handsomest young men to see them. It worked once in a while, but then again that buyer didn't stay on the job very long because she wasn't profitable.

In the same sense anyone who hires a young woman as a salesrep thinking to "sic" her onto a male buyer is asking for business trouble. That buyer has to account to cold, hard figures which come up every three months. You and your young woman rep are going to get nowhere unless she can deliver quality and price and delivery of the product. If she doesn't know what she's talking about, the buyer will very soon realize you have been trying to make a fool out of him. In the end you will have accomplished nothing more than making the buyer take a very negative attitude toward you and your business.

Most of us—men and women—have been too exposed to the movie version of the high-powered woman executive wrestling with a sense of impotence and then going back to fulfill herself (whatever that means) on a ranch in the country.

The high-powered male executive, on the other hand, is supposed to go on to the end, fulfilling himself by dying for the company.

That kind of thing was always for the birds. But romance has a way of clouding reality. If you look into business history, you will find that some of the greatest merchant houses were administered by women. It was only beginning with Victorian times that, romantically, women executives became "special." But they still ran the farms in the South and businesses in the North!

Now that companies and sales agencies have had more experience with women as numbers on their sales charts, they have come to realize that treating them in any other way than as business associates is more than stupid; it is unprofitable.

How do you train a female sales representative?

Like everyone else.

As you do for everyone else, you have to determine: Is she cut out for the free but self-disciplined life of a salesrep? Does she really like to meet people? Is she hungry for money? Will she be around long enough for your training investment to pay off?

If you find she can't make it . . . fire her just as fast as you would a young man. It's for your good as well as hers.

If she has it . . . make sure she keeps that initial enthusiasm by seeing that she gets what's due her . . . in money and prestige.

There is no "special" way of treating or training women salesreps. They either have it or they don't.

That's why everything in this book applies to women as well as to men—as principals, as reps, as buyers, as agents. There is no point to seeing it any other way.

Either people in business (men or women) are profitable . . . or they're not.

SHALL I HIRE SOMEONE WHO MIGHT STEAL MY ACCOUNTS OR PRINCIPALS?

A whole library could be written on this subject. But it would all boil down to this: everyone knows, or should know, his own potential. If you don't, get away from everybody for a day, sit down in unfamiliar surroundings far away from telephones, and assess yourself.

1. I was tough enough to go into business for myself (one of the toughest decisions of your lifetime).

2. I am succeeding. (This is true when you have been in business for three years and your real income has risen two years in a row. If your real income has remained static, you are not succeeding.)

3. My list of accounts and principals is expanding. (Account expansion should always be more rapid than principal expansion. Your greatest asset is your list of accounts. Without it your principals won't want to know you exist.)

4. What is my object in deciding to hire someone? (Wider coverage? More concentrated coverage? Continuity? Which do I need most?)

5. Am I taking this step only because of principal pressure? (They always want more coverage. So do you—if it can be done profitably.)

6. Do I have enough cash in the bank to cover a rep's expenses for a year?

   a. How much will it really cost you to put a junior on a salary, or on commission and expenses, as a business cost? Remember, it will be at least a year before the payoff on a junior begins.

   b. How much of your own time is it worth to put on someone with experience as against an untried novice?

7. Could I reach the same objective by spending the money on promotion?

   a. If the promotion were successful, wouldn't you need someone just to cover the leads?

   b. In your field, has promotion had one-third the success of personal selling?

If you have been in business successfully for three years, you are a good rep and have the instincts that make for survival in business. If you take on an experienced rep who can wean away a good principal, that principal was about to go anyway.

The real question you have to decide is: Will you dilute yourself among your own accounts if you do not put on someone to cover the wider territory your principals demand?

Principals do not usually change reps who are expanding. They begin to look around only when they find their markets are static or growing smaller.

HOME OR OFFICE ADDRESS—PRESTIGE OR ECONOMY?

Wouldn't it be more profitable for me to work out of my home as against an office address? Think of the money I'd save.

How much prestige would you lose?

In the Orient the word is "face." We call it "prestige." You can't measure prestige with a ruler. But without it neither principals nor accounts will have much confidence in your lasting ability.

A live person answering the telephone sounds a lot better than a mechanical device. This person can answer questions as to when you will be calling, and may even be able to call you if it's an emergency.

Of course, you don't need an office in the beginning. For paperwork, files, etc., you can work out of your own home. But an answering service at an office address, which will also take care of your mail, makes you look professional—someone who's really in business to stay.

You hope to move into an office someday.
Point right to it from the beginning.

WHAT ELSE BESIDES SALES WILL KEEP YOUR BUSINESS ALIVE AND HEALTHY?

The first thing is your personal health. You are your business' first and greatest asset. That's why a physical every six months is the best investment you can make.

The rest you've heard 5,000 times, but it's still true. Mismanagement of overhead and expenses has ruined more businesses than lack of sales.

Try and think of it this way.

You have a lot of invisible partners. But the one who demands an exact accounting, with payments four times a year, is the Internal Revenue Service. IRS (hereinafter called *"them"*) has the power to make you very uncomfortable. You have to satisfy them or you are not going to stay in business. They say they want only what the law says they deserve. *You* have done all the hard work, so you want to make sure you get everything that's coming to you.

Because you want your business to be around for a long time, you're going to make sure it gets everything it needs to stay vigorous and healthy. Use the IRS reports you make as checks on how you're really doing. These reports have no sentiment and no excuses. Use them as warning signals when you see yourself going off the track on expenses and overhead.

The following is a partial list of things you should do but often slough off.

1. Keep the best on-the-run records available. ("I do. I do." Then why are so many reps always down for an IRS audit?) Any stationery store will sell you an expense notebook. It should be in your car . . . or in your briefcase. Don't keep it at the office or in a safe desk at home. That's how it gets lost. That's why entries are forgotten. If it's too big to carry, get a slim monthly book which you can keep with you.

2. Save every receipt. ("All that paper!") When taxes are due, and you have none of the receipts which would mean an extra $2,000 or $3,000, you'll wish you had bought one of those inexpensive tin receipt files. ("All that paper" now turns into "money in the bank.")

3. Have your business car or cars serviced where the service station keeps mileage records. Independent audits of mileage can save your business enough to pay for their maintenance.

4. Besides your credit card receipts, keep a log of lunches and entertainments in your daily expense reports. One checks against the other.

5. You keep a record of your calls anyway. Keep a duplicate for "them." "They" like records which prove each other.

You've known all this since you were twenty-one, but your records are still no good.

Try to make them as automatic as possible. For instance, in Seattle you can buy access to a bank's computer. You put a template over your telephone and punch in your daily expenses and other tax data. At the end of the year you get a complete readout for tax purposes. Imagine how records like that, verified by your own logs, would look when you go to your friendly IRS auditor and she says, "What have you got to back all this up?"

Whatever else you feel you can do better than anyone, **do not do your own tax return!** You may be the best rep on two feet—your sales forecasts the most irreproachable, your handling of customers superb—all that automatically makes you a rotten tax accountant.

It's worth the fee (which is deductible) just to prevent you from spending a costly week with a friendly IRS investigator.

But make sure your tax expert is an accountant who has been in business and will keep your tax records year after year. You get what you pay for, and in this case going to a store-front "expert" is like going to a quack who will charge 50 percent less than a surgeon. You pay less and lose your right arm.

Telephones are the lifeblood of your business. Make sure they are used for business. There is a fiction around that says, "Oh, charge it to the business. No one will know." Overloading your business with expenses can give it heart trouble.

Your other expenses, such as rent and stationery, are up to you. A business address and a telephone answering service are necessary expenses. Suppose your office telephone is in your home. The line may be busy for hours. Or how will you feel when a buyer tells you he called and your small daughter answered?

Make sure your commissions are correct. *Paid sales* are the lifeblood of your business. They are "paid" only when you are paid the correct commission. In these days of erratic computers and adding machines whose transistors are slightly worn, all kinds of mistakes can occur. Check those commissions every month. If one is outstanding, though you know the invoice has been paid, do not allow sixty days to go by before you have queried your principal's accounting department.

Stapled to the copy of every order which has been sent to a plant there should be a copy of:

1. The acknowledgment

2. The shipping notice

3. Any correspondence on the order

4. The invoice

These should be held in the open file. If the file is still open after sixty days, query your principal about your commission. If the invoice has not been paid, that will be your signal to move in at once and find out why. There may be something wrong you don't even know about—something which might affect your relations with the account.

Have someone else go over your commissions as a check. After all, if you sell $400,000 a year and there is a $\frac{1}{2}$ of 1 percent error, that's $2,000—the money that is the lifeblood of your business.

HOW DOES A SMALL, BUSY BUSINESS EXPAND?

We're a small business working all the time just to keep up with present accounts and principals. How do we expand?

There is no such thing as a permanent plateau in business. You either go up or you go down. By staying with exactly the same group of principals and accounts, you are asking for something to happen. When you've been on the plateau too long and the inevitable occurs, it will take a lot more effort to get back up to where you were than it takes to keep that graph climbing steadily.

Try to make a presentation to one new account every other week—not just a pitch, but a presentation which will require at least one hour.

Have a full-dress review of your line at least twice a year. What do you need to make it more complete?

Can you spend one working day a month (preferably at the end of the month) looking for new accounts?

Doing something different—seeing new people—going to trade shows—these things break the mold of custom and make you think differently. Looking for new business is the one activity which challenges the mind and keeps it open to all new eventualities.

It also means more profitability and a greater diversity for your business.

PERSONALITY CLASH

"I should hire this salesman but I just don't like him."

Be unique.

Hire on the basis of "How much business can this guy bring in now and in the future?"

Everyone likes to work with people like themselves. That is what is really meant by "I like him." You recognize this salesman as someone like yourself.

It is only the unique sales manager who hires a man he doesn't like personally because that man can run at a profit in a very short while. You take on a salesman to help you reach your profitability goals. He is not there to be a social companion, someone you can talk to, a reminder of your youth, or even a golfing partner.

Hiring someone you don't "like" may be the best thing for you. It enables you to view the man's work and your goals for him impersonally.

Even if the decision falls to a man you do "like," it's a good idea every now and then to ask yourself, "Suppose I couldn't stand him; how would I think he was doing? Would I put up with the way he's handling his accounts?"

That's how you get an objective view.

It's a good idea to give yourself the same treatment once in a while.

PIONEERING: IS IT WORTH IT?

There is a well-respected line you are considering taking on. It will take years to pioneer. Is it worth it?

Forget the glamour. Look at it from a profitability angle.

1. Knowing that pioneering the line will be taking up a lot of your time, can you handle it profitably?

2. How will your present principals react?

3. Is it worth it in terms of:

   a. Money?

   b. Experience?

   c. Your getting into new accounts because of its prestige, thus benefiting your overall sales?

4. Will the manufacturer pay part of the way?

   a. Manufacturers know that if they get a large firm to represent them, the firm will put them on the bottom of the list and wait for orders to come in. That's why they're interested in you in the first place.

   b. If it's to be a long haul, will they finance your out-of-pocket expenses without expecting exclusive attention?

5. Will they merchandise for you?

    a. Go into regional shows?

    b. Do mailings in your name?

The questions you have to solve are these: Is it worth it in the long run? Can you afford it in the short run?

SHOULD YOU DIVERSIFY?

Lots of companies, a lot larger than yours, are finding that the diversification road runs down as well as up.

1. It's fine on the way up.

2. One or two bad decisions, in a field you don't know, have a tendency to magnify trouble because you do not have the expertise to rectify them in time. It's a very rare occasion when you can hire or even recognize that expertise. Ask any conglomerate.

In your case diversification can be very appealing. The argument is: "Sure, I cover the material handling field; but suppose that dies off? Wouldn't I be smart to be in printing because (assign your own reason)?"

If you have a lot of money, you can start two companies: one in material handling and the other in printing. Install two presidents while you chair both boards. This is like the advice the doctor gave to the man of thirty-two who had a wife, a mortgage, and five small, hungry kids: "Spend the next four years taking it easy on some tropical isle. It will do you a world of good."

Diversify within your own area of expertise.

Someone always needs something in your field. Make sure they call you for it.

Make sure you can get it for them.

SHOULD YOU HELP FINANCE A SMALL MANUFACTURER?

Inside every rep's mind is this small dream: "Brother, if I were boss, I'd show those dummies how to run a plant."

But before you help take on a manufacturer's labor worries, plant overheads, taxes, market research, etc., think about several things, and think hard.

1. Is there such a demand that you can't lose? Or will this demand have to be created?

2. Does it call for your own expertise, or is it a field you know about from hearsay?

3. Are the manufacturers putting everything they have in this world into it? Or are they letting their friends in "on the ground floor"—which may only lead into the basement?

Remembering that great salespeople are always the very best prospects for a fast line, consult your accountants. If they don't stop you, go and see the coldest-blooded bankers you know.

Ask the question that provides the acid test: Without your credit rating being involved, would they make a loan on the business itself?

CONSUMERISM—DOES IT AFFECT YOU?

Yes. No matter who you are or what you sell, consumerism does affect you. It always has.

Consumerism will turn out to be the best thing that ever happened to American business. Faced with demand for quality as well as quantity, business will turn out both without going to the artsy, craftsy extremes some people would like to wish upon it.

If you handle any item that ultimately finds its way into the hands of the consumer, you are going to be held responsible. It doesn't matter how many exemptions have been signed for you.

Recently, a manufacturer and its advertising agency were sued by FTC and FDA for falsification of claims. Note that the agency was included. It had to pay an enormous fine because nowadays the "should have known" principle has become a legal factor. The agency contended that they merely used facts supplied by the manufacturer. It did them no good at all.

Therefore, if you are selling a component going into, say, nonflammable baby garments, you had better put a match to a sample in front of witnesses to show that you have tested the part.

The same thing should be done with spot samples.

And, in spite of all this, you had better be covered by liability insurance in case someone "proves" that your component would have caught fire if the garment had been thrown into a burning building at two in the morning.

But, more than that, if you plan to be in business five years from now, you should make sure that everything you say your product can do, or your plant can make, is in the realm of reality. The $500 commission you made from plant A selling shoddy material can wipe out $8,500 worth of commissions on reorders of a good product.

Quality of product and quality of word have always been the bases of fortune in the rep business. No matter what you see on smart TV programs, the lying, cheating con artist is usually finished in a very short while. Anyone who makes a success that way proves the product is a lot better than they are.

Moreover, the moment competition is represented by someone reliable, the successful con artist is dead.

YOU WANT TO ANSWER A "BLIND" AD, BUT WHO IS THE MANUFACTURER?

Is it one of your principals looking for someone else? Is it a manufacturer you don't want to represent? Is it another agent on a fishing expedition?

You can write through an attorney. But this is never very satisfactory. The advertisers will know that the letter is only looking for information. They may not even want to answer.

Some businesses keep a hidden address (usually a post office box) and false stationery. This is all right for getting competitive information. But suppose you use it to answer an ad and the advertiser turns out to be someone you·would like to represent? How do you explain your actions without leaving yourself open to suspicion?

It is possible to write a letter and then enclose it in another envelope addressed to the magazine itself with a note: "If the box address is for the ―― Company, please throw away this letter." This allows the magazine to keep the advertiser's name secret.

But make sure the periodical will do it. Some newspapers and magazines will not forward *any* mail which restricts their actions. If by some chance the note to withhold has been disregarded in their offices, the periodical leaves itself open to court action if it forwards letters which it was not supposed to forward in the first place.

Then you never know if your letter was sent at all.

The best method is the telephone. If it is your own principal, you must know someone there who will tell you "on the side." If it is another manufacturer, someone whom you want to represent, call them and ask. If it's someone you don't want to represent, call *them* and ask. You don't have to follow the inquiry up. But using the telephone in these cases saves time and worry.

THE MANUFACTURER WHO IS NOT REPRESENTED IN YOUR TERRITORY

This manufacturer's products are well made and excellently priced. They'd go right along with your present line. On the other hand, if they are not in your territory, it may be that it isn't profitable. In that case, if they took you on, you would be merely a sideline, to be dropped when things are good.

However, it is always best not to think that everyone knows everything about your territory the way you do. The sales manager in this company you would like to represent may have just decided to start looking around in your territory for a rep.

The best idea is always to present yourself and see what happens.

Of course, you know the sales manager's name. If doing that isn't worth a phone call, the company isn't worth contacting.

```
Dear Mr. Pfaelser:

We call upon every well-rated ratchet user
in the Tri-State area, as well as smaller
companies whom we know to be volume users and
good payers.

We were impressed by the products you dis-
played at the ISSU show, from both the value
angle and the merchandising standpoint.

If you have been considering this territory
for expansion purposes and have the capa-
city to satisfy it, we'd like to talk to
you.

Please call and we'll set up a date.
```

A "FAST-MOVING" PRODUCT OFFERED BY ANOTHER MANUFACTURER'S REP

You have been offered a chance to sell a "fast-moving" product in your territory. Drawback? It's being offered by another manufacturer's rep who says he is acting as distributor. *You are going to ask a lot of hard questions before you take this one on:*

1. Are you building up this other rep to a point where as "distributor" he gets to know your accounts as well as you do? It may well be that after a year or so you won't be needed any more. This has always been a favorite method of breaking into new territories.

2. Is there enough in this offer for the very short run? (An offer from another rep is very rarely good for the long haul.)

3. Is the other rep feeling his way toward making an alliance with you? (Chains of reps who can offer a manufacturer strong representation in many parts of the country within a short time have unusually strong bargaining positions.)

4. Is this offer okay with the manufacturer? Will he stand behind you as well as his usual rep?

5. Of course, the main question is: *Who* is going to pay you, the manufacturer or the rep? If it's not the manufacturer, you may have trouble collecting. You will certainly have trouble with complaints.

6. Is the rep being pushed for wider coverage than he can efficiently give right now? Sometimes smaller reps will look for someone else to "help out" while they are growing or before they can become a link in a chain. Have it out with the rep who's inviting you. Don't pussyfoot around. If the rep remains evasive and can only give big promises, forget it. If you are only going to be a pioneer, forget it. You'll be doing it only so someone else can reap the big rewards.

But if it's fast money for the short run and you can easily work it in with your present line, go ahead.

Develop a competing manufacturer whose line you can pick up in a hurry when the rep you are "helping out" suddenly finds he doesn't need you anymore.

SHOULD YOU LET YOUR PRINCIPALS KNOW ABOUT THE NEW LINE YOU ARE THINKING OF ACCEPTING?

1. Especially your big profit makers. The others won't care.

2. Your big profit makers may not wish to be associated with the new account. They'll let you know why soon enough. Through them you may discover things about your new line you would never have known until you became associated with it.

3. On the other hand, your principals may also be impressed. Being courted by a new principal may make them realize more than ever what a winner you are.

There are some things you should be secretive about:

1. Your accounts' blueprints and sales strategy.

2. Anything your accounts tell you in private.

3. The same with your principals' blueprints and strategies.

But being open otherwise with your accounts and your principals gives both a good feeling about you—especially if they never learn anything about their competition from you. If you talk about someone else, they'll know that you're shooting your mouth off about them.

HOW MUCH DO YOU PAY WHEN IT COMES TO ADVERTISING?

1. Consumer advertising:

Nothing.

Everything, if you are acting as a distributor and packaging under your own brand name. Of course, here you try to get the manufacturer to go for a percentage on the theory that increased sales will lower the overhead. This is never successful in wearing apparel; it is sometimes successful in a food preparation that has a high profit margin. It has also been successful in hardware.

2. Industrial advertising:

In this we are taking for granted that you are acting as a manufacturer's representative.

a. MAILING. You never pay for the plates or the printing.

Since this cost is spread over all the manufacturer's territories, he always bears this cost.

If it's a mailing job: "We're only doing it for you," the manufacturer still gets most of the benefit and there is never any reason why you should go for these costs.

b. BROCHURES. If you are making up a brochure for a mailing to all your accounts and prospects, your principals will usually supply you with cuts, halftones, logos, etc. It has sometimes—but not very often—happened that they will even pay a part of the printing cost. Usually that is done under conditions which will annoy your other principals. When a manufacturer pays, he will want *your* brochure to feature his name and products.

If a principal is making up a brochure and he is going to have your name imprinted (not rubber-stamped), the cost of imprinting is sometimes (very rarely) shared. If your name is going on the brochure from the start, it costs no more for the principal to have your name imprinted.

If the manufacturer is supplying the list and all the answers go to him to be parceled out, there is no reason why you should pay. If you are supplying the list, it is best for you to do your own mailing. Why give out your account list to someone who will in turn sell it over and over again to list companies in an attempt to get back the cost of their brochures?

GOING BROKE IN THE "SMALL, RICH TERRITORY"

"I know of one manufacturer's representative who sells to only five super-large plants. When this rep takes on a new principal, it is understood that these five plants are the rep's sole territory. The rep doesn't care who else is sold in the physical territory, or by whom, but those five accounts must be protected. Is that smart or is that smart?"

It looks wonderful. The rep is selling only to the rich. They must know they will get superb service and that they will be well taken care of personally. *They* have it made . . . for as long as they want.

But does the rep? If there is enough money to be made in the very short run, that rep has it made, too. But look beyond the very short run. Key-account buyers must recruit new sources all the time. If they don't, outside controllers (besides the internal auditors) will look cross-eyed at all those orders going through one agency. They will begin to see shadows on the wall.

Even if that doesn't happen, suppose one of the principals decides to give the line to a rep who has been doing a terrific job in the rest of the territory. Can any buyer drop the manufacturer just because "a friend" no longer represents the account? What kind of memo can the buyer write explaining why GCE (a fictitious name) is "no longer one of our suppliers"?

In the long run this rep is the loser. When the boom is lowered, that will be the end. The rep will have to start all over again. That is the toughest part of the whole deal.

TRADE SHOWS—HOW IMPORTANT ARE THEY?

Everyone pooh-poohs them, says, "Never again," and shows up year after year.

1. If one of your principals does not invite you to participate—to be at "the booth" when a show concerns your territory—prepare to find another principal. Being at the booth is that important to you.

2. Let all your accounts know that you're going to be at the show. Tell them to look you up. Not only will it add to your prestige; you'll be surprised at how many of your accounts will be glad to see a familiar face.

   You will also be in a position to explain to the purchasing agent and the engineers or production people all about the product while it's right there in front of you.

In *regional shows* consider taking a booth for yourself and displaying all your lines.

1. In this case *you* are running the booth. Your principals' names are subordinate to yours.

2. Confine yourself to shows in your own region. There's a lot of waste in cooperative booths at a national or seminational show.

3. Your principals will usually be glad to help you set up your own exhibit.

After everything is said about having your own booth, the main thing about it is the fact that it raises your status. Your accounts come by your booth, shake your hand, and say, "Hey. You're right in there." They like to do business with someone they feel is right on the ball.

Principals (present and prospective) feel you're someone they want to reckon with now and in the future.

The aura of progress and success is worth all the money you've spent on the booth.

It's tax-deductible, too.

LOYALTY—TO WHOM?

Loyalty has its own priorities. The first one is to your family; the next is to yourself, then to your business, third to your accounts, and finally to your principals.

You are loyal to your accounts because without them you have no business and no principals.

Through your efforts your principal is one of their sources of supply. But if you are ever in a position to offer your account something better—a new time-saving product, or a better value—this is something you have to do because the account is your prior loyalty. Besides, competition will make sure that you do.

Your loyalty to your principals consists in informing them of new needs, new products on the drawing board, competition's moves, and account necessities. You must also try and protect them from bad credit risks.

Your loyalties make you keep your eye on the future. Your present principal (or principals) in a certain line may be bought out by a conglomerate. The new heads may decide to change their sales strategy so that you are left out in the cold. Some other agent may talk them into canceling you. A principal's first business loyalty is to the plant—not you.

That is why you attend trade shows, talk to the competition, write letters, and keep a high profile. You have to think ahead if you are going to keep those first three loyalties happy.

FORECASTS—ARE THEY A WASTE OF TIME?

Only if you don't use them.

Only if you don't use them correctly.

There's no need for you to do elaborate graph making or economic forecasting. These have all been done for you by:

1. Your trade journals

2. Newspapers

3. Local business-conditions letters sent out by your bank

You also know what's going on because you're around all the time listening—to buyers (who are usually pessimistic), to other salespeople (who are usually optimistic), and to your principals (who try and straddle the fence).

What should be your stance? Frankly, it's best to see the bright side of things. First of all, you want to give the impression that you're going up all the time. Secondly, you don't want to get the reputation of being a "Gloomy Gus." Cassandra, the bringer of true but gloomy tidings, is rarely a welcomed visitor, except among the bankrupts.

You should also get to know some people in the financial world. They get all their reports from Federal Reserve forecasts, but their knowledge of local conditions and local accounts can be of enormous help.

Now, how do you apply all this information to yourself, to your business, and to your income in the near future and in the long run?

1. Is the number of factories (or accounts) in your area growing?

2. How many second shifts are being put on among your own accounts? How many in your territory?

3. Are your own orders rising or falling with the average in your territory? In your industry?

4. Are you getting your share of the orders in your territory? The goal, of course, is 100 percent. Fighting for each order is the best way of ensuring your own position.

Don't be discouraged by bad financial forecasts. The world, according to the bankers, is always about to slip off the precipice. Somehow it never does.

The two graphs you do need are for stimulus only. One is for gross sales; the other, for sales by principal. These are your most important indices, and they should be going up.

That other important record, your bank statement, is the best financial index of all. Useless worry about the world merely puts it on Weight Watchers.

The rep who pays too much attention to broad indices will always be surprised to find that competition has been getting rich while he worried.

TAKE TIME OUT TO COMMUNICATE WITH YOURSELF

You know how to talk and write and run for your accounts. You knock yourself out making sure your principals know what's going on.

But do you ever communicate with yourself?

Do you ever sit down, preferably away from home and the office—send your family away for the day—and think things over—objectively, as you would do for one of your accounts? As you would do if one of your principals asked for a survey? As you would do if you had a sales manager who asked you to investigate someone else's territory?

What are your goals for the next year? For the next three years?

1. Income. Not some impossible figure like 500 percent, but a steady 10 to 20 percent increase and how to get it. Are you going to need more principals? A new salesrep? Expansion outside your territory?

2. Accounts—new and old. Who should be concentrated on in depth? Who is taking up too much of your time for what you get out of it? We all know there are accounts where, for some personal reason such as not liking the buyer, we don't concentrate and therefore we lose a lot of business.

   We all know also there are accounts where we spend too much time because the buyer is fussy or can never look ahead more than thirty days. On the other hand, we may just like the buyer—have "a great time with him"—so that account gets a disproportionate amount of effort.

3. Sources—old and new. Are you missing anything from your line that can become a steady source of new income? In the daily rush are you overlooking the fact that you are going to be in business five years from now and that you should be planning that far ahead?

4. Has your overhead taken a sudden leap that you can't account for? Are your selling expenses too high? Have business lunches and entertainments become expensive social affairs?

5. Have you been missing accounts because you don't have the time—or think you don't?

6. Have you been taking more and more time away from selling in order to concentrate on paperwork—because it's so "necessary"?

7. Could a product that isn't selling be weak because you haven't pushed it as you have a product you like to sell?

It is during these fews hours of detachment that you can throw off the dross of old thinking and decide on new approaches. By self-searching you can find out or decide on what you did wrong in handling an account or a source and decide how to get it back.

Communicate with yourself. The easiest thing in the world is sloughing off a problem when you're busy with something else. But when you're alone and there's no one and nothing to distract you from unwelcome self-criticism, from business you handled wrong or amateurishly or even spitefully, that is when you lay the foundation for righting yourself and pointing all efforts to the profitability goals you have set.

But don't do it too often . . . usually not more than once or twice a year. More than that, and you become a prey to self-doubts that have no basis in facts.

SUCCESS CAN BE THE SUREST WAY TO FAILURE

You have had two or three good years in succession. You know that nothing can go wrong from here on in. It's not that you do nothing . . . or even slow down. It's the tenor of your work that has begun to change. You begin to give more attention to paperwork. You begin to believe the old wives' tales that no one ever really wants to see you on Friday or Monday. You rely entirely on the telephone or even a letter, instead of going out to see a customer who is annoyed or who is only a small lug in the big chain of command. What the hell, you know the boss; so what can any buyer do to you anyway?

This is the point where you are now most vulnerable. Success breeds fat and easy ways. It opens the way for the lean and hungry competitor. Remember how you were when you were hungry? Nothing was ever too much trouble. No one wanted to see you too early . . . or too late. It was never the wrong time.

"Hell," you say, "I'm no different now."

But aren't you?

Have you begun to notice that you are not getting the trial R&D requests you used to?

You hear, "We have to get someone else in here. Just for the small stuff you don't want to handle anyway. It looks better." This from the younger buyers—the ones who have to make their own names.

Have you noticed you are not getting the small orders which invariably lead to the big ones? Could that mean they are trying someone else out? "You wouldn't want to handle these little stinkers." Does it mean they think you are getting too big to give them the service they want?

Threshing motions, incessant paperwork, and surveys of surveys are no substitute for work. They just make you feel you're doing something on a wet day when you don't really want to go out.

Check your last month's calls.

You may find that you are averaging only one "important" call a day. Three years ago you were averaging three. Look at your routings and see if you are not just riding around so that you can be near home, or the office, or the golf course at 2:30.

Sometimes you'll have to shut the radio off. You have been late at quite a few calls because of a tight inning.

It's very easy to fool yourself into thinking you have been working productively.

It's impossible to fool that cold-looking bank statement which comes in every month and tells you fair and square exactly what you have been doing lately. Some reps fool themselves by saying, "It's been bad before. It'll soon be better."

After a while the word "never" can be substituted for "soon."

YOU WANT TO RETIRE IN FIVE YEARS

You've been active in business all your life.

1. You want to phase down but not out.
2. You want to phase out entirely.
3. You want to phase out gradually but retain an interest in the business you built up.

What is the disadvantage that looms largest?

1. You have nothing material to sell but a name.

There are other disadvantages. Perhaps you only rent space. Office equipment can be sold at only a nominal profit.
What is the big advantage?

1. If you have been in business more than ten years and have had a successful career (everyone assesses "success" differently—but if you have been in business ten years, have survived on your own income, have some money in the bank, and have a list of good accounts—including the key accounts you handle—you can count yourself successful), **you have a name and reputation** to sell.

2. Your name can lure good principals ("I've known that outfit for years; they have a good reputation" is a powerful magnet) and accounts ("they've been doing business with us ever since old Allison was an assistant P.A.").

A good name is an invaluable asset. Ask any national advertiser.

Start thinking about what you are going to do five years before you do it. Forced sales never bring in the money they should.

1. Talk to your lawyer (if you have one). Talk to your

accountant (you should have one—it's the best way to get an independent valuation of the business).

Talk to your contact at the bank. This is very important. It always surprises people to discover that bankers can find investors for their particular needs. But that is why they are in business. That is why it's always a good idea to establish contacts with your local bankers.

2. What do you talk about?

    a. When the time comes, should you offer the business to the present employees as a stock venture with yourself heading up the board?

    b. Should you offer partnership to one or two key employees who have done very well with you and for you? (Your accountant should be able to give you an independent appraisal of them.) Don't rely entirely on your own appraisals—they're apt to be biased.

    c. Should you sell out entirely right now to another firm that's offered what you feel to be a good deal? Watch out for stock offerings whose value will be determined after a three- to five-year period. By that time they have your accounts and your principals. They can set their own valuation on your business. It won't be high. A manufacturer's rep agency should be sold for cash on the barrel head.

    d. If you have decided on the first two alternatives, should you start the changeover now or within three years of your goal?

It's impossible to say which is best for you. However, it's a sure bet that unless you can keep some kind of control, you will be treated like every other pioneer—exploited and then ousted.

In the end every agreement depends on the people you pick. If you intend to rely solely on a piece of paper, remember that the words "but they signed a contract" have been uttered by many saddened men and women.

If you allow your key people a chance to get into the act "profitably" as soon as possible, your chances of phasing out and keeping control are a lot better. While the weight of gratitude is nil, the thought that you could always ruin the business by taking away your name and contacts can weigh very heavily when the inevitable "Why not dump the boss *now?*" discussion comes up.

Another way of phasing out easily is to keep close hold of your direct key accounts—the ones you are handling right now. Place the responsibility for new accounts and principals on the key people who are going to take over. This will make the business—and you—more valuable.

Being chief executive is most effective when you have four or five people—key people—each of whom has stock. This enables you to act as ambassador to the senior buyers at key accounts. Yours also becomes the enacting signature with new principals. This kind of action allows you to call your own timing. You go into the field voluntarily, which means the pressure on you goes way down.

Anyone who has been active for years—as any rep is bound to have been—has a tough time adjusting to total retirement. Everything turns dull when there isn't the constant spice of involvement to tone up the system. If you are in basic good health, phase out in such a way that you'll be needed for a long time to come, in a sales and marketing capacity.

CHAPTER TWO

Your relations with your key accounts

THE VITAL PART OF YOUR BUSINESS

Nothing in business is more important than your relations with your accounts . . . especially your key accounts.

Without your accounts you are nothing.

Without your key accounts, your best principals won't want to know if you are alive . . . and why should they? Without accounts, you represent a dead loss to yourself as well as to them. Without key accounts you are only another rep to be replaced when someone better comes along.

Your principals *are* important, but only secondarily. One of your better principals may, from time to time, remind you how much money you have made handling his line. He will take pleasure in pointing out to you how important his firm is to your well-being. Smile and nod. But always remember that without your accounts, you wouldn't have made a dime. Without your key accounts, the principal's sales manager wouldn't be having you out to lunch today at the country club. Without your key accounts, that sales manager wouldn't even be talking to you!

That's why this book stresses key accounts—the big profit makers: how to get them; how to keep them; what to do when you lose them.

Nothing like this is done with your principals in mind for one very good reason. When you have good accounts—key accounts—you soon have very good principals.

When a salesrep for a large company is covering a key account and doing it very well, sometimes the company decides it wants to transfer the rep. They offer "promotion" to other and greener fields. Smart reps think five times before they accept. They ask themselves: Is the company bringing in someone else, a relative perhaps, to handle my old territory? Are they telling me that "loyalty" to the company demands that I get out there and develop new territories without compensation?

Sometimes, especially in smaller companies, management cannot bear the thought of someone not "in the family" controlling an account which can mean so much to their volume.

If this is you, make sure those new fields really are greener. Loyalty goes down as well as up. Think about what will happen if the same pattern repeats itself. Will you be bringing in the big ones and getting the prestige while someone else gets the money?

As was pointed out earlier in this book, prestige without money is an empty success. You can get all the awards in the world, be pointed out as one of "our best people," have everyone slap you on the back—but the proof of that prestige is how much money there is in that check at the end of the month. Top salesreps don't see the carpet on the floor of their offices that often, anyway.

This is where the manufacturer's rep holds the upper hand. The key account knows him—not his principal. Of course, the rep brings in officials of the companies he represents from time to time. But it is the rep who is making introductions. He is the one handling all communications. He is the one who develops his accounts. He is the one who has gotten his key accounts out of binds.

He gets the full rewards of his labors.

Buyers are human beings. If a manufacturer's rep has done a good job, they won't be happy with a principal who tries to cancel out the rep for no good reason. A buyer will want to try out the rep's new principal just for old times' sake.

So when you handle a key account, hold on to it and cultivate it the best way you know how. It's the only substitute for a money tree a manufacturer's rep will ever find.

BREAKING IN—THE RIFLE BEATS THE SHOTGUN EVERY TIME

Why do they need me?

What do I have to offer which they don't have now?

Do I have a product which is unique?

Is there anything in my line that no one else makes? . . . Anything we make better? . . . Anything at a better price?

Do I have a name—or a new process—they can exploit in their promotion?

Do I have the service? Can I get my product there faster than the competition can? Will my shipping costs be lower?

What do I have that offers an unsurpassed value—something I can pound on with the buyer?

These are the things you have to find out from research.

What exactly does GCE (a fictitious name), the account you want to gain, do? What does that specific plant—that specific division—make? What do they specialize in? What are they "famous" for in their own eyes?

GCE Locks and Gauges Co., Inc., may just be a carryover from the days of "our founder" one hundred years ago. Nowadays, "everyone knows we are the foremost fabricators of electronic pulse switching devices." Make sure that "everyone" includes you. The buyer will soon have you out of the place if you try to sell parts or fabrications for locks and gauges.

You have to go in with an idea . . . a plan which will be profitable to GCE. That's why you do your research. Get a corporate report if GCE is a public firm. Libraries have copies of state and county industrial directories. You may have access to a D&B report. If the company advertises (industrially or consumer-wise), see what they've been selling for the last twelve months. If they sell through distributors, the advertising will let you know.

All these reports and ads will tell you what the company does. The local directories will tell you what GCE makes at that specific plant. It will tell you how many employees it has there. Don't trust the information which gives you the name of a specific buyer. When you're dealing with a key account, that information is often out of date.

Call the plant. Ask for Purchasing, and tell them you wish to make a presentation of your product to the buyer. Don't be mysterious. It is the buyer's professional obligation to see you. You might have something new.

In another part of this book there is a section of letters which have proven successful in getting appointments with "tough" buyers. Your telephone call should be a synopsis of one of these letters when the buyer asks, "What do you want to see me about?"

What you will be saying in reality is: "I have a plan (or a product) which will be extremely profitable to GCE." The rest is a garnish of sociability.

The appointment is made.

Many times you won't be seeing the senior buyers at first. They're too busy. You'll be pushed off onto a junior. Remember this and take advantage of it. The junior wants to fight his way up. If it's a woman, she is trying to make a name for herself fast. Privately they are sure the senior buyers aren't doing half as well as they could if given the same chance.

Try to be the one who is going to be the vehicle for that chance. Show the junior buyers that you want to help them rise. Pick out the one item in your line the buyer can use—the one product of value you know has some superior claim. This is the item you feature.

These young buyers don't have all the time in the world, either. They have all the mean jobs pushed onto them: reports, statistical work, cost coordinating—everything the senior buyers hate doing. They don't have the time, or the experience, to go into your whole line, and you just want to get on the books.

The younger the buyer, the more respect you should show for

the position. Reps who treat younger buyers with a condescending "I'll show you what it's all about, kid" usually get nowhere in a hurry. Young buyers are so busy resenting them they take pleasure in saying, "We already have five good suppliers in your field, but you can never tell. Just leave your card and maybe we'll. . . . No use leaving brochures at this time. Our files are overflowing."

On the first interview you will, of course, give a fast, sketchy background of yourself (because it's really you that is being sold), and then present that one hot item. You'll go into that in detail; and because it is only one item, you can sell it in depth.

Trying to sell your whole line during the first interview only creates a fog through which the buyer has to peer to decide whether there is anything in there the company needs . . . and whether you are the type of person they like to do business with.

Why should a key-account buyer take the trouble?

Make it easy. Present only one item at the first interview. It makes you and your line easier to remember.

Of course, you'll always offer two brochures—the other one is for the relevant department. The buyer won't have time to read it, but the brochure is a tangible reminder of you. What you want to stick in the buyer's mind is that you are offering a line the buyer's plant really needs, plus one item of value—something that can be recommended at the Thursday morning production meeting, something which will get the buyer noticed favorably by management.

Then you'll write a letter telling what you've done, timing the letter so that it arrives on the buyer's desk three days later . . . though never on a Monday.

It won't happen that easily.
It rarely does.
Not at a key account.
Some buyers have personal policies; they won't even allow you to quote them (let alone sell them anything) until you've been in five times over a period of six to eight months. Buyers then feel

that the rep is in earnest. And you have to have a good reason for coming in each time. This is another reason why it is a very bad policy to spill your whole line during the first interview. "Got anything for me today?" will be a dirge to your hopes.

Watch whom you ask to lunch. These days some companies look askance at a rep trying to take their juniors out on the first try. The junior may feel you are pushing too fast —trying to take advantage of lack of experience. Unless you are accompanied by someone who knows them well (your principal may be taking you around to several accounts with whom he has done business in the past), senior buyers are rarely asked to lunch until they have first done business with you.

It may take five to seven calls before you get that first request for quotation. It may then be only for a fill-in. How you handle that first request will be of interest and will be closely watched.

If your quotation is not going to be on time, let the buyer know in time and by telephone. Make sure you have a positive reason—"the estimators are making new time studies so that we can give you a more realistic quote."

If requests are handled badly, how will you handle orders?

Be eager for the business and show it. Some reps make the mistake of acting as though they were above everything. They theorize that if they act as though they don't want the business, they won't be accused of pushing for it if anything goes wrong. But buyers misinterpret reasons like that. They feel that the rep is only "going through the motions" because his principals don't really want the business. Nowadays "GCE wants suppliers and agents who are really concerned." The rep who doesn't show real interest and enthusiasm won't be given a chance.

There are little human things you have to watch for. Many buyers will lecture you on what they and their plant need. Make sure you are listening intently. The buyer is telling you something all the research in the world won't give you: the plant's real troubles, how you should slant your quotes. Do you actually have a chance right now? The buyer is telling you that if you can solve any of the plant's problems, you're really in.

Be an apt pupil when you are being instructed by a buyer or

any of the production people. There isn't a soul in this world who doesn't want to teach somebody "everything it took me years to learn." If you can become his protégé, you're so much further along.

You don't know everything. You never will.

No matter what your age, show them you want to learn so that you can help them.

Get to know the production people—the people who can use your products. With the buyer's permission (make sure they always know what's going on; no buyer—or anyone else, for that matter—likes anyone who goes around his—or her—back), get to know their headaches and their gripes. You'll save yourself a lot of hassles on returns and rejects.

Know the production people, and you'll soon get to know when orders are about to happen.

Buyers in a key account get to change as frequently as every two years. That makes it incumbent upon you to get to know every buyer in the place—and their assistants and their secretaries.

Anyone who doesn't know that secretaries should be well treated is cutting business effectiveness in half. In a key account, secretaries are the "keys." They are the ones who can make sure you get all the requests for quotations with the right information. They can arrange quotes so that yours looks favorable. They will slip you the word if your prices have been getting way out of line. They will tell you the best day to see the buyer. ("Don't make it next Tuesday. You'll only get a fast hello. There's a budget meeting on Wednesday, and they all have to make recommendations for next year. Why not make it Thursday after the meeting is over?")

Think of all the time you could have wasted.

Whether she is a Weight Watcher or not, every secretary should at least get a box of chocolates at Christmas time. A secretary certainly is worth it.

Your first order is usually a test order in more ways than one. How is it going to be handled? Will delivery be on time? Will Quality Control pass it through?

All the imponderables will be riding on that first order, including the buyer's judgment. Will this agent turn out to be a dud? Is this a responsible principal the order was placed on?

A buyer is allowed only so many lapses of judgment.

When that first order is being produced, anything that can go wrong will! Everything seems to be against you: a crucial machine breaks down; truckers go on strike; the factory can't get its hands on the exact material required.

Should you inquire, "Will GCE accept a substitute?"

Your answer is usually a resounding "No!" because you don't want to ask. ("A helluva way to start a relationship!")

But if you explain the trouble, the buyer will usually send you to someone in engineering or production. If the substitute is close enough, engineering or production will, in a majority of cases, say, "Sure. We were considering that anyway."

If they say, "No," the buyer will usually give you a time extension.

The strange thing is that even the buyer instinctively expects something to go wrong on the first order. That's why you got only a fill-in in the first place.

The only thing that must be absolutely right is quality. If the order goes through Quality Control without a hitch and if the late delivery (which is usually the trouble on a first order) doesn't hold up production, you can begin to probe deeper into the key account.

Life will never be easy handling a key account. There will always be emergencies, new buyers, engineers who want you to turn the machines upside down for a $100 order, accountants who want you to get your principals to change their billing methods to "bring them into compatibility with our computer," research people who want impossible samples, etc.

But at least you will be well paid for your trouble.

KEY-ACCOUNT BUYERS: YOUR JOB IS TO MAKE THEM LOOK GOOD

Small-account buyers usually have other duties as well as buying. Such a buyer may be the purchasing agent, accountant, and office manager all rolled into one. The buyer may be the owner. It may be someone in production who's responsible for keeping the plant going while the boss is out looking for business. Buyers in this category push for a price; but as long as you've done well by them in the past, they are not going to make life any harder by going out and looking for competition. They are "seat of the pants" buyers. Don't look down on them because of that. Most of the time, they do very well indeed, because they are close to the final product.

Key-account buyers have to have a different outlook.

How they purchase makes or breaks them. They are specialists, and a lot more is expected of them.

If they are wrong too often, someone will soon say, "Goodbye. You are a nice person, but we just can't afford you."

Like the policeman's, the buyer's lot is not a happy one. If something good happens, the buyer rarely gets the credit. Production or engineering or someone will be sure to step in and say, "Yep, we did it all by ourselves. Purchasing? They just bought what we told them to."

But let something go wrong, and it's always the buyer's fault. Then Production shakes its collective head and says, "We *told* them to buy the KRE spec, not the HUR. . . . HUR was on the requisition? Hell, they still should have known better. It was just a typing error, and we can't catch everything inexperienced secretaries do. We *told* purchasing often enough that it had to be the KRE. They should have called us and made sure no matter what the req said."

You, the rep, are one of the very few means by which a buyer can gain promotion, raises, and status. Advance word of new machines, cost-cutting methods, and lower prices which can spell profits or loss to the company comes only from you.

You are, therefore, one of the buyer's main keys to success. If buyers aren't sure of it, one of your first jobs is to convince them of the fact.

That is why in key-account selling, **it is your job to make the buyer look good!**

Think about it for a moment.

At first glance is sounds like the worst kind of brown-nosing.

But is it? The truth is that when you make a key-account Buyer look good, you are:

1. Doing a good job for him . . . or, in lots of cases nowadays . . . for her.

2. Doing a good job for the buyer's company.

3. Doing a good job for your principal.

Most important of all

4. You are doing a good job for yourself.

Making the key-account buyer look good is the highest form of self-interest.

Each buyer is a different individual. Each one has to be sold differently. All of them have their private foibles and prejudices. But if you keep one thought in mind: *you are setting out to make this buyer look good,* you have the right psychic force working for you during your interviews. It doesn't matter whom you are selling. No attitude will better enable you to withstand changing buyers, different policies, changes in principals, etc.

Make the buyer look good.

It's the one attitude which can get and hold key accounts for you better than any other method.

DOES THIS BUYER . . . ?

This is the most delicate question in the sales field. Sooner or later you'll be faced with it. Since time immemorial there have been rumors of key-account buyers who had to be paid off.

Ninety-nine percent of the time the rumor starts with a disgruntled salesrep. How many times have you yourself said, "There must be a payoff," when you've lost a particularly lucrative order on a close quote.

When these rumors have some truth to them, the culprit is usually caught by the internal accounting people. By looking at invoices and comparative costs, a good comptroller can usually spot any appreciable difference faster than anyone else. If the comptroller misses it, the outside auditors (who have access to the records of many of the same types of businesses) begin to wonder out loud at the fact that such and such items are being bought 5 percent higher than average industry cost.

Or it sometimes happens that the Vice President—Purchasing begins to ask, "Why haven't we more competition in here?" The sticky-fingered buyer gets frightened and gives business outside the payoff circle. Then one of the long-time payers gets angry and spills the beans, thinking he's been "double-crossed."

Even if you are tempted to get into the payout line, forget it. It's usually a very short-term proposition with long-term side effects.

1. You can be sure it will become known. When it does at a key account, everyone who has been a substantial supplier to that buyer will be out in the street "pending investigation." That can take three to five years.

    If you have been a substantial supplier and have gone the straight route, it will be necessary to seek an interview with the Vice President—Purchasing and ask to have your books audited by an outside, impartial firm. This is the only way to relieve yourself of the general suspicion.

2. Small and fill-in suppliers are usually not touched. If you have been only a standby supplier because you never paid off, now will be your time.

When a buyer is on the take, it gets known throughout the industry faster than it does to the delinquent's own company (on the principle that the husband or wife is the last to know). Buyers in other key accounts are then afraid to do business with the suppliers of the delinquent buyer because they don't want to get tarred with the same brush.

So anything you have gained in one place will soon be lost in another.

There is another long-term loss: anytime a certain name is

brought up by a junior buyer, some senior will say, "Weren't they implicated in that bribe thing with what's his name?" Then they'll tell the junior, "Better lay off. They've got a very bad reputation."

You might as well go out of business.

In the new consumerism you may even be brought into court to pay back whatever the buyer was paid plus damages.

Paying off is a very short-term advantage and always ends up unprofitably financially, morally, and status-wise.

In an economy which works on credit—and the integrity of your word—it cannot be afforded.

PRESENTATIONS

Tell Them What They Want to Know!

CASE 1

You are making a presentation to the buyer alone and by appointment.

This means the buyer has set aside an hour of valuable time to review your entire line . . . or some aspect of it which has become interesting for company purposes. You do not know what these purposes are, but to make sure you take full advantage of this interview,

1. You have brought along enough samples and bro-chures—one for the buyer and one for every relevant department. If there are two departments which can use your products, bring along three sets of everything. Department heads will very rarely borrow someone else's brochure on the chance he may find something "hot."

2. If it is to be a graphic representation with time studies, slides, and motion pictures, make it short. You are not a movie producer. We'll devote part of this section to this type of presentation.

CASE 2

This presentation is to the buyer *and* the production, engineering, or systems department. At least, they are going to have someone present. Make sure you know exactly what it is they want to know more about BEFORE THE MEETING. Buyers are usually glad to pass on the required information. They are not interested in wasting everyone's time.

Usually the other people at the presentation (beside the buyer) are interested in only a certain aspect of your line. If you are going to try and sell everything, you'll soon lose their interest; they can't use it anyway.

After you have gone thoroughly into what they want to know, you can mention other items you think they should know about. If you raise no spark, don't push it any further.

CASE 3

The product calls for a high capital expenditure.

The capital projects review board of GCE (our fictitious company) is interested. The buyer who brought it to their attention feels good. This is the recognition every buyer hopes for.

Now it's up to you.

It has been decided by you (consulting the buyer), after a survey, that GCE can use twelve of your machines over a period of five years. Cost will amount to over $1.5 million.

Think about getting the chief engineer of your principal's plant to come along with you when the presentation is to be made. You may be stuck with the sales manager as well, but the chief engineer is the important one. The sales manager can do only a trifle better than you. But in the eyes of the capital projects review board, the chief engineer is "one of us." He talks the same technical language as the board members. He most likely graduated from a school they know well or went to themselves.

You don't use someone like that for opening interviews—a buyer would feel you were trying to overwhelm him. The chief engineer should be held as a "big gun" for just such presentations as these.

Visual Presentations

Too many times companies and their representatives get lost in the stars when they make visual presentations. They have forgotten that buyers and engineers have seen so many of these that after a while they inwardly groan when someone lugs out a reel, asks for an outlet, and says, "Your eyes are going to pop when you see this one." Maybe they will and maybe they won't.

If you have been in the army or navy, you will remember that "orientation film time" gave you some of your best naps.

Keep to your subject and try to remember that x-rated movies can be seen anywhere.

Try to do something individual. A certain rep was having a terrible time selling a labeling machine with the movies the manufacturer had provided. They were good movies technically but out of the same slick mold as a thousand others. They did a swell job featuring models in mini skirts but they didn't sell the machine.

This rep took "home movies" of an application on a production line. The backgrounds weren't very good, the picture was slightly out of focus (in fact, it was 'way out of focus), and the product glared because of the amateurish lighting.

But the rep was able to give such a graphic account of the application (everyone also got a laugh at the "I'm not exactly Cecil B. DeMille") that the point of the film—the machine—went over big.

The rep began to sell machines.

It was the excitement over the new labeling machine that got into the motion picture the rep was showing. There weren't any pretty girls. The machine took over the glaring spotlight and sold itself. At one point in the picture the machine ran out of labels because the operator had been staring at the camera.

Perhaps this presentation was better because it was not a slick professional job which pointed up the talent of the director and the actors. Buyers in key accounts see these films all the time. Sincerity is not so prevalent a commodity.

The Follow-Through

CASE 1

Without exception after every presentation a letter should be written recapping what you said and, if possible, giving prices and terms. It does not matter than you left brochures. It doesn't matter that "everyone" has your card and has promised to call when you are needed. It does not matter that you think the whole thing was a flop and you feel that you'd better think about doirg something else for a living.

Follow-through is the most important thing in life, love, sports, and sales.

NOTE. Always leave or send at least two of everything: one for the buyer's files, one for the relevant department. If you leave or send only one, it may go into the buyer's files alone. That will do you no good, since it's the department which is going to use it that has to make the requisition in the first place. How can they send in a purchase order or a requisition if they don't know about it?

CASE 2

To the buyer who gave you some time. You do not sell him.

Dear Mr. Andrews:

I want to thank you for taking an hour of your time to go over PCV's line of ratchet heads. The factory has just come through with two new sizes (or new prices—or authorization for a trial run—or discount for new users—or more favorable terms). I am enclosing two sets of

these new ratchet head specs so that you may
have them in your files.

I'll give you a ring next Thursday (a week
later) so that we can discuss the matter
further.

If it looks very good, you'll be in the GCE neighborhood next
Thursday anyway so that you'll call for an appointment.

CASE 3

You presented a certain part of the line to the purchasing agent
and a production department head. The letter, of course, always
goes to the P.A.

Dear Mrs. Anderson:

Thanks for the time you and Mr. Roberts gave me
Thursday morning. Those "home movies" would have
been longer, but, like every other amateur, I ran
out of film.

Since my return I have talked to my plant about
a test run. They are willing to supply you with
a short run of ratchet heads, at the quantity
rate, so that you can decide for yourselves how
much of a time reduction, as well as a cost reduction, you can effect.

I personally feel the number of rejects will
be down considerably as well.

Since I expect to be in the neighborhood one
day next week, I'll give you a ring and we can
discuss the matter further.

CASE 4

You and the P.A. have reviewed the line. You are selling them
right now, so you went to work on what he doesn't buy. You do
the same in your letter.

Dear Mr. Patterson:

Thanks again for allowing me to show you our entire line of ratchets and holders, cams, and power spacers.

Cams and spacers are being used by more and more barbell manufacturers because of the ultimate savings they make on the production line. The initial installation and breaking-in period does look expensive in terms of overhead at first glance. But that cost is soon overtaken and passed by a positive reduction in the number of rejects and the eventual elimination of six hands on each line.

Attached you will find statistics from the Barbell Manufacturers Institute which prove the point to a certain extent. I say "to a certain extent" because you and I know there is no such thing as a "typical business." The eventual overhead reduction in this "typical business" is shown to be 14 percent. I think even a 6 percent reduction is something to conjure with nowadays.

As I said, and can now confirm, we will be happy to help you with a pilot program. We think it will quickly lead to a full installation.

I'll give you a ring next Thursday to see if I can clear up any points which may have been brought up since our meeting.

Yours truly,

NOTE. Never be too enthusiastic about statistics. Most buyers know, or believe, that they can often be "fixed."

CASE 5

The entire capital review board was there. The letter, of course, goes to the P.A. with whom you do business. If the Vice President—Purchasing was there, he does not get the letter.

Dear Ms. Rogers:

Mr. Chas. Sweeney, Chief Engineer of RCVP Products, and myself want to thank you again for the chance to present our RCVP Rotating Head Ratchet to the Capital Review Board.

Mr. Sweeney told me, after we left, "Those people certainly know what it's all about." He said he hadn't been questioned so thoroughly since he went up for his Doctorate ten years ago. Incidentally, I'm glad I didn't come alone!

Should the Capital Review Board desire an on-the-job test of the RCVP, we will be happy to make our newest model available, send along our usual instruction team, etc., and treat the entire matter as if we were making a permanent installation. However, we will allow you to try the RCVP for a six-month period. Our only conditions are that you pay for freight both ways and for the out-of-pocket services of our technicians if you decide not to go through with either a purchase or a lease program. If you do, regular charges will apply.

I am sure the capital projects review board will welcome this chance to make a definitive test of the RCVP on home grounds. As your Mr. Reston said, "How do we know this will work for us, under our conditions and in our plants?"

This trial period should provide the definitive answer.

I'll call on the third for your decision in this matter.

Yours truly,

NOTES. Never offer anything for nothing.

Always compliment personnel. Privately, they may think "Mr. Reston" is a dummy, but that opinion is to be held by insiders only!

DISAPPOINTING KEY ACCOUNTS AND EARNING THEIR GRATITUDE AT THE SAME TIME

You have one item which a key account wants "exclusively" though only in a small volume "to try it out."

You want to get as wide a distribution as possible because you know that competition will be on your tail, and soon. *Therefore you have three problems:*

1. The territory being asked for "exclusively" is a good one which promises lots of volume.

2. The principal is demanding action *now* . . . and can demand it because of this product.

3. The key account is one of your best, whose hostility may cost you lots of money because right now he buys everything you sell.

WHAT EXACTLY ARE YOU GOING TO DO?

1. You can't straddle this fence. It has to be one thing or the other. You decide that this key account is so important you'd rather lose the money you could get by selling the product all over the territory. You'll stick with the account. If you do this, make sure the key-account buyer, the vice president of purchasing, and everyone else knows what you are doing for them. Let them know that the principal will be cutting you off or perhaps selling direct. Remember also that gratitude is not an extensively used commercial credit.

2. The decision is: you are going to sell as widely as possible. A lot is riding on this product: top commissions, recognition as the agent who has been picked to sell a big success, and new key accounts you will be able to sell whom you could never get near before.

But, for the sake of the future, you are going to have to

placate this key account who wanted an "exclusive." They deserve some consideration. They just about put you in business.

How do you disappoint them—in a way that may make them grateful?

1. Get the law on your side. Your customer knows that restraint of trade, even indirectly, can bring you both into court. Make it plain that his firm would hate you if that happened.

2. Have someone at your factory, preferably the president, send you a signed directive stating that all accounts in your territory must be called on within thirty days or they will make the offer themselves by mail with no commission to you.

After presenting these arguments, tell your account you have found a way to give them a jump on everyone else legitimately. Tell them you will place their order so that they will gain at least two weeks over competition.

You are not breaking any law and you are serving a good account. Shipments on items like this are on a first-come-first-served basis anyway. Other territories have to be serviced as well as yours. Place their order at once. It will be at least a week or two before you get any others.

Even the appearance of cooperation will often convince your key account that you have done the best you possibly could.

Many times we exaggerate, in our own minds, an account's potential hostility. If they have been an especially good customer, we tend to worry even more. But when a key account is shown that we have tried, and are trying, but just can't make it for them legitimately, most of them are human.

They go on to the next problem.

YOU "KNOW" YOU JUST DON'T HAVE A CHANCE

You "know" that "old Peterson," the buyer for GCE (our fictitious key account), "always gives" this type of business to Barbells, Inc. It's going to be a big order, but you "know" you've been put on the list only out of courtesy. Why should you bother to answer the request for quotation?

BECAUSE YOU NEVER "KNOW"!

1. You never know! Barbells, Inc., might have become so cocksure of themselves that "old Peterson" is suddenly confronted with a 10 to 13 percent difference in price.

2. You never know! "Old Peterson" may be annoyed with Barbells, Inc., for some reason you'll never even hear about.

3. You never know! Production may be "sick of those damn Barbells people. They've been sending in too many rejects. Isn't there anyone else in the field who can quote on our requirements? What's the use of low prices if the value isn't there?"

4. You never know! Barbells may have known someone "inside"—a production clerk, perhaps—who gave them details no one else could get. The production clerk has now moved on.

If the cost of quoting is going to be expensive, call the buyer. Tell exactly what the quote is going to cost your principal. Ask if you do have a chance. Buyers know what costs are. That's their job. They'll tell you whether or not your quote is just a formality.

If they say, "Quote," write a preliminary letter saying your factory is going to quote: ". . . however, it may take a few days longer than the deadline set for returns."

This lets GCE know that you are in dead earnest.

Then quote.

Because you never do "know"!

Announcing the Fact That You Are Going to Quote

The preliminary letter announcing the fact that you are going to quote is like an overture.

It sets the stage.

It tells purchasing that someone is going to come on strong— that before any decisions are made, there may be a new star. "Watch out for us!" is what you are saying.

Because this is an official letter, you do not mention the phone call you made to ascertain whether it was worthwhile or not. That was a personal matter between you and the buyer.

```
Dear Mr. Peterson:
     Thank you for your Request For Quotation
PN 72956.
     My plant tells me they are going to sharp-
en the pencils on this one because they want the
order.
     However, the estimators are going to have
to make some new time studies in order to refine
their costs. They tell me that this may hold
them up a couple of days.
     Our formal quote may therefore be in a few
days later than October 23d. It will be in no
later than October 26th. This will in no way
hold up delivery beyond the 12/5 request date.
     If possible, I will give you the price by
telephone before that time so that you will be
able to weigh it against other quotes.
     Again, we appreciate your thinking of us
in this matter. We also want to thank you for
all the business you have placed with (or
through) us in the past.

                              Yours truly,
```

A YEAR INSIDE AND . . . NOTHING

"I've been inside this key account for more than a year now, and all I get is emergency orders and fill-ins. I think I'm kept on the books because the buyer has to show there are other sources on tap. Do I drop it?"

The question is, of course, academic. Very few of us can afford to drop a key account, no matter what, because of the potential.

In some key accounts it takes as long as three to five years to become established.

First of all, there is the routine. "Barbells, Inc., usually gets large opening orders. They've been doing it for years." Unless you are radically lower in cost than they are, you will get only the fill-in business to start with.

Secondly: There is always a long probation period. Can you deliver what you say you can . . . time and time again?

In the depth of your discouragement, remember that in dealing with a key account, time is on your side. Every two or three years the buyer is usually transferred to other products or moved to another division. A new buyer comes in, and there is your chance.

1. You are an established supplier.

2. You have produced fast shipments for the company. The buyer is going to need fast future shipments.

The new buyer will have no prior friendships or commitments. He—or she—may not know that Barbells "always" gets the large opening order. If you have treated the secretaries and assistants right, they may not even tell him.

In a key account everything changes—except the need for good service. When you're "in," you have a continual selling job to do, which keeps you on your toes. When you're trying to get in, you get a new opportunity every two or three years.

This is true of volume business as well.

DEAD END?

"But this is no fun. We've been into this key account for four years and there still isn't a smell of volume. We still get only the

fill-ins and have to fight like blazes for them. Is it worth it?"
First some questions:

1. Is your principal (or are your principals) giving you the proper cooperation? Should you look around for a new principal who will strain hard for the volume business this key account can bring?

2. Have you brought any new ideas into this key account in the last two years? Or has frustration built a wall around your brain? When you stop bringing ideas to buyers, you become just another body calling on them. You're not helping them in their quest for personal advancement.

Okay, you've done everything possible, but you know you won't get volume for a long time. The present supplier, for some very good reason, is "in."

1. You don't give up. You do reduce the time spent on the account. You make appointments so that you work the call in between other interviews.

2. You answer letters.

3. You answer requests for quotations.

4. You point out the emergency deliveries you have been making.

5. You *do not give up.*

You are always on tap in case there is a change of organization, the buyer leaves, purchasing becomes decentralized or centralized, your competition fouls up, or the thousand and one other things occur that make business fascinating.

You may have to face up to the fact that the present buyer just doesn't like you personally—you know, that often happens.

The rewards for persistence in hanging on to a key account can be enormous.

They are worth the effort.

GETTING AND KEEPING CREDIT FOR A "RUSH"

A key account needs a rush delivery.

You know for sure the "rush" is necessary. A line might close down if the material isn't there on time. It doesn't matter whose fault it is. Justice (or the fact that the buyer's computer didn't work) has nothing to do with it. You have to pull the buyer out of a hole.

You also want to get credit for your effort.

First you call the sales manager at your principal's. Even better, call production. Tell them your troubles. Offer something. Tell them they can put this emergency job into production ahead of one of yours where the need is not so great. Trading puts you in a better position and lets the plant know how important this delivery date is to you and your key account.

Follow up with a memo at once. Phone calls can be conveniently forgotten.

```
FROM:  You           DATE. . . (same as phone call)
TO:    A. J. Meister (Production)  RE: Job 78314
                                       GCE

Dear A. J.:

Right after I got off the phone with you, GCE
called me to make sure those ratchets would
arrive on Tuesday, the 17th. I told them you
had personally assured me they'd be going out
via air on Monday night and that I could pick
them up at the airport Tuesday morning.
     A. J., it'll mean a lot to us right now
and in the future because, if they don't get
this shipment in time, GCE will have to close
their line. That's at a cost of $10M an hour!
     Thanks a lot for all the trouble you're
going to, A. J., and don't forget to push back
that other job if you have to.

                              Thanks,

                              You

cc: C. F. Peterson, Purchasing
    GCE.
```

By sending the buyer copies of your memo, C. F. Peterson is able to reassure production. The implicit promise of "in the future" has a better chance of being kept.

THE SMALL THINGS

In these days of computers not only does everyone want their invoices on time, they also want them made up in a certain way. If you don't follow the rules, you'll find the accounting people complaining to purchasing. Small complaints like this can add up. Take the static off from the beginning.

```
TO:     Your controller
FROM:   You
Dear Ruth:
Please make it a standard rule to have all of
GCE's invoices sent to them in quadruplicate.
I know it's extra work for us, but the buyer
tells me we'll get our money at least ten days
faster if we follow their rules.
                                          Rog.
```

You'll find your own accounting people always feel their way is best and you should "educate" your customer. You have enough trouble *selling* GCE, so give your accounting people some kind of reason to follow the rules. Sell them.

CHAPTER THREE

Your relations with your principals

The most important determinant in your business is: yourself. What you do—and how you do it—determines the course of the business in the long run and the short run. If you don't handle it correctly from the start, there will be no long run.

The second most important determinant is your accounts—especially your key accounts. The way you handle them and the way you handle yourself are so tightly interwoven that it is often hard to discover where one leaves off and the other begins.

The third most important determinant is your principals: who they are, how you get them, the way you handle them. (The whole thing revolves around you.) A good sales rep who has nothing good to sell is a farmer with no fields, an astronaut without a ship, an order taker without a sales book.

You need good principals as much as they need you.

"Baloney," you say. "They can change me any time . . . and they will if they ever get a chance."

"Baloney," the principal replies. "That rep will jump to another manufacturer who offers him $1/2$ percent more than I do, given half a chance."

If a principal puts out products at a good value and you have good accounts—key accounts—you then have an equal relationship. This is something you both can build on.

There are certain times when you need a principal more—as

when an account needs a rush job or a bit of research the cost of which "we'll put into the final price."

There are times when they need you more—when the backlog is low or they are putting out a new product which needs a special push.

Just as much diplomacy and salesmanship is necessary in handling principals as in handling accounts.

It is well to remember that the superior need will change from time to time. You have to think of that and prepare for it in advance.

Principals' first loyalty is to their own businesses.

Your first loyalty must be to your accounts . . . the mainstream of your business.

That is why you sign contracts, or letters of intent, with your principals.

THE PRINCIPAL AND YOU: WHAT ARE YOU BOTH LOOKING FOR?

Your time is your most important capital asset.

You have two important goals for it:

1. Investing it to the utmost profitability.

2. Making sure that no one but you fully owns it. The moment your time is owned by someone else, you are working to maximize their profit. That was one of the reasons you went into business for yourself.

You know that, in order to meet your profitability goals, you must have good accounts—key accounts. But the best salesman in the world is going nowhere unless he has the right principals in the field he knows best.

So what are you looking for in a principal? *Preferably* one who:

1. Is small with a unique product.

2. Is well financed but not so well financed that the company is ripe for a takeover.

3. Is not about to consider your territory a fringe area to be mined when business is bad and forgotten when business is good.

4. Is run by an individualist who doesn't want to be gobbled up by a conglomerate. Sometimes principals with super-egos will burn you up, but at least you know they (and their excellent product) will always be there.

5. Believes in giving good value as a sound business investment.

6. Is a professional who is interested in solving customers' problems.

7. Regards you as an important profit center.

Of course, these seven points represent an ideal. No principal is that perfect. But if you get one who has four out of seven of these points, hang in and give the best service you can. You'll both do very well.

Three out of seven is an acceptable average.

YOU ARE JUST STARTING OUT

You are looking for principals who make the kind of product you can sell because:

1. You have the necessary expertise in the field.

2. You know the buyers in the field. (This can be 50 percent of the expertise.)

You are looking for a principal who is an energetic producer with whom you can work.

YOU ARE ALREADY IN BUSINESS

Your needs will, therefore, be slightly different.

1. You are looking for principals whose products add to, or complement, the lines you already carry.

2. You specifically want manufacturers who can help you with your key accounts.

3. You want principals who are hungry for profitable business and want to stay in business!

4. You want principals who pay commissions on time.

PRINCIPALS LOOK FOR REPS BECAUSE

1. They are dissatisfied with the market penetration their present agents are making.

    a. The present representative may be too big. "I'm on the bottom of their list. They don't 'sell' my product. They just sit there and take orders that come in over the transom."

    b. The present agent may be too small. "They do all right, but they don't *go* anywhere. Oh, they get some business, but if they'd only get the lead out . . . I keep telling them there's gold in those other accounts, but they just don't listen."

2. The rep hasn't sold any of the key accounts in the area. "Oh, my agent's okay on volume, I suppose. But just look at the ones they don't sell—GCE and all the other big ones—the volume users." The big account you don't have always looks better than all the others put together. The smart rep uses this atmosphere to get the kind of terms which will ensure penetration into major key accounts with the manufacturer's product.

3. "I happen to know that J. B. down the road, my chief competition and a rotten producer if I ever saw one, is getting lots of business out of that territory. How come they're into GCE and I'm not?"

    Again, this is the kind of atmosphere the smart rep uses to get favorable prices and terms.

4. "That agent gets business, but I don't know ... I just don't like them." Someone else was sales manager when the agency contract was signed. No one can do anything about personal antipathies. Look around for another source.

5. The principal is looking for *expansion* into new territories which look like logical markets. In the consumer fields, such principals are the ones who are usually looking for agents. In industrial fields, it is usually the rep who sells the principal on the new territory. If this principal has the production facilities, he is positively your best prospect.

Most rated small manufacturers are represented in their home territories by their own people or by themselves. This home territory will always be basic for them—the one they serve first because it means bread, butter, and better profits. If their capacity will not go beyond home territory during "rush seasons," you will have trouble when your accounts need product.

In most cases you'll be only second best.

If the manufacturer is covering the home territory during the rush season with only one shift, this means he can readily expand to a second shift. That means an increase in output of 80 percent; second shifts never mean an increase of 100 percent in production.

Once your key-account work comes in volume, your principal will have to put on a second shift. Can he afford it? *Will* he afford it? No matter what anyone tells you, factory people will not work overtime forever—even at time and three-quarters. Besides, their efficiency goes 'way down after they've worked ten hours.

If your prospective principal is a small business, try to find out who the owners really are. Is the president the owner or merely the figurehead for interests that want to sell out as quickly as possible? See if you can get a Dun & Bradstreet (the usual D&B) report on the company. Have your bank check the company out with its friends. See if people in your trade think it is going to be in business for at least ten years (barring accidents) so that you can have something to build on.

Make sure that prospective principals pay their bills. A slow payer can mean a fight for every commission check. Anyone who has been in the rep business for a time can tell you hair-raising stories about manufacturers who feel cheated every time they send out a commission check. "That rep only sold it. I had to produce it . . . at a loss!" the moan always goes.

Sign a contract.

If anything happens, you will at least be covered.

Representing a middle-sized company is the best way to go.

1. The company has the capacity or the financial background to build upon when and if it is needed.

2. The company has the necessary plant to do research work, or to have it done for it, when one of your key accounts is looking for a new application.

3. The company can do some market research work for you. In fact, try and stop it. You will be bombarded with all kinds of propaganda and requests for paperwork "to enable our experts to reassess your particular market." But at least you know the firm is aggressive. You know the company will fight for every order because the owners want it to grow.

There are drawbacks here, too.

1. There is always the chance that the owners, or their families, will take the conglomerate route. The new owners, of course, will bring in what are known as "modern managerial techniques." This will mean that the computer has shaken its head when your territory was run through it.

2. A new sales manager may appear with a change of heart: "This territory is now built up to where we feel we need

100 percent of a producer's time." Since you shake your head, you are out.

This is why you must always keep contact with new suppliers and new principals. This is why loyalty to your business comes ahead of loyalty to your principals.

This is why you sign a contract: so that you can get six months to change or to develop a new principal.

Then there is the big corporation, or one of its divisions. There are numerous reasons why it would use manufacturer's reps instead of its own salespeople.

1. The product is a sideline which looks profitable. However, the marketing people have come up with the determination that their own sales overhead is too much for the product's small potential. Therefore the owners will let reps sell it with the thought in mind that once the product becomes profitable and pays back the original research costs, they will be able to sell it to another corporation at a good markup.

   The other corporation may not need reps.

2. There will be some products that can be sold at an excellent profit in certain areas where relevant businesses are concentrated. Outside these areas the number of prospects is too thin. The corporate decision is then made to use reps in these "fringe areas" so that the profit picture for the rest of the country will not be disturbed. After a while, if it is shown that the reps are doing well, they can always be replaced by the company's own people.

This is not to say that a big company is not good to represent. If the product has ready sales, it will furnish income and prestige, at the same time helping you to get into new key accounts. It will also serve as an excellent reference with new principals. "Hell, if they're good enough to represent GCE, they're good enough to rep for us.

Sometimes these relationships have lasted a long time. But most of them last only as long as the contract—or until the accounting group comes to a new sales manager and says, "Look, at this volume we could be selling product X for $8\frac{1}{2}$ percent cost, and you're paying these reps 10. That's a clear $1\frac{1}{2}$ percent loss." Everyone will shake his head and you'll be told, "We wish to take this opportunity tó commend you for the fine work you have done for us in the past."

"In the past" are the operative words here.

As before, this is why you signed a contract in the beginning. It gives you time to develop a new principal.

The principal and you are looking for the same thing: help in meeting profitability goals. You need his production know-how. He needs your sales expertise.

HOW MANY PRINCIPALS?

New reps often wonder: "How many principals do I need to do a good job?" The question should be, "How many principals do I need to give my accounts the best value and service?" "Okay," the new representative will answer, "what I really want to know is, how many principals do I need in order to make money?" The answer is still the same: In the rep business, it's the one who delivers value on time who's going to make lots of money.

So a rep needs as many principals as are necessary to cover the field.

It is possible for you to be in a field where you need only two or three principals to give complete coverage. You may also be in a field where you need thirty principals.

The new rep will say, "Thirty principals! I'd get all mixed up trying to sell thirty different products."

You would if you sold that way.

A rep doesn't think in terms of principals or their lines; he thinks in terms of product categories. No one can do a good job selling "lots of products." Anyone who tries that will end up selling nothing.

The smart rep reacts first of all to needs. He fashions the sales interview to meet buyers' wants, switching from product category to product category. The interview will begin with the rep stressing something unique—or timely—thus creating a new need. If that fails to raise a spark, the rep falls back on the familiar.

That's why a rep can have thirty different principals and not get mixed up.

What you *must* know are the products you are carrying in your line and all the ways your accounts can use them. That way you serve your accounts best, give your principals an even break, and end up doing very well for yourself—which is the measure of the whole thing.

LETTER TO A PROSPECTIVE PRINCIPAL

You Are Just Starting in Business

Of course you have found out the name of the sales manager of the company you are going to write to about representation. A letter addressed to "The Sales Manager" is like an intimate personal letter addressed to "Occupant."

You have also made sure that the sales manager won't be away on a six-week trip—in which case your letter would be held for all that time at the bottom of a pile.

How do you find these things out? Pick up the telephone and call.

The letter is short because you are looking for an interview on a matter where everyone profits. This is not a job application. You are independent—in business for yourself.

Write on a letterhead. Otherwise, you look like an amateur who is nervously nosing out the lay of the land.

Dear Mr. Schweitzer:

    The northern Ohio sales territory is wide open for the sale of barbells right now. I can deliver these sales to you from customers who

```
can make solid gains on your sales graph now
and in the future.
      Let's discuss the possibilities. I'll give
you a ring on the 15th and we can set up a date.
                              Yours truly,
```

Sure, the sales manager wants to know who you are, etc. But don't put any of that in the first letter. You can do it all at the meeting, when you give your background, your experience, and what you hope to accomplish. It's during that meeting that you give your enthusiasm full rein; that's when you show the sales manager that getting onto *your* team will be the most profitable thing the company has ever done.

You Are an Established Business

You are an established business with two or more reps in the field. You can offer wide coverage as well as depth.

```
Dear Mr. Schweitzer:
      We are three seasoned sales engineers
covering the northern Ohio-Michigan terri-
tory. That means you can get 21 years of
successful selling on your side at once,
provided your product is one we feel can
profitably be used by our many fine ac-
counts.
      Just make a list of the twenty biggest
volume ratchet users in this territory. If
we aren't selling seventeen of them, your
list is out of date.
      If you will call me, I will be glad
to set up a meeting so that we can pursue
this matter further.
                              Yours truly,
```

You are a trifle arrogant. You should be. Where else can they find a successful sales force at once?

Answers to Box-Number Ads

A letter in answer to a blind ad (a box number) in the *MANA Journal, The New York Times,* or your own business periodical should always be written on a letterhead if you want to be taken seriously.

In answering blind ads, it is not necessary to start your letter: "In answer to your ad in the＿＿＿." They know where you saw the ad by the address.

If it is not a blind ad, remember that you are selling your services, and the magazine, or newspaper, is selling its own readership. Therefore, at the bottom of your letter in the P.S. position write, "Answer to ad in＿＿＿."

The ad read:

> Representative for northern Calif. Outstanding barbell ratchet manufacturer opening new protected territory. Modern facilities. Own engineering dept. Well rated. Good commission basis. Answer Box XXX

THE ANSWER

```
Gentlemen:

        I am able to offer you the in-depth ser-
vice you need in the northern California terri-
tory. I have called upon barbell ratchet users
for the past four years. I know who to see, what
they use, and how quickly they pay.
        If your product can stand up to quality
specs and you can make on-time deliveries to
this territory, I am sure we can make a connec-
tion profitable to both of us.

                              Yours truly,
```

When you put some of the onus on the principal, he realises that you mean business and are not just interested in handling any old line. You have stressed quality and promised accounts with good credit. You are offering a "profitable connection."

The personal interview will be time enough to go into your qualifications—your previous record. If you are a new rep, glory in it. Never apologize for anything. After all, you can offer physical vigor, a knowledge of the territory, and a real desire to work hard because you're hungry.

That first interview is the time to demonstrate your enthusiasm. It is better to go overboard at that time than to be cautious. Cautious salesmen rarely do anything spectacular.

Who knows, you may even reach the estimated sales figure you give the sales manager at that first interview.

HOUSE ACCOUNTS—HOW TO HANDLE THEM FROM THE START

A principal wants you to handle his product or line with "certain exceptions"—which always turn out to be "accounts we've sold for years." These are sometimes divisions of large corporations which are to be handled separately by "our own sales manager" or "centrally." "We have contacts with headquarters."

1. Decentralization of buying has been growing by leaps and bounds. Divisions in your territory may be tied to central purchasing only for policy reasons. More and more, each local purchasing agent has "responsibilities to their own division which is now a designated Profit Center." Translation: The P.A. doesn't buy through H.Q. anymore.

2. Without the house accounts principal wishes to withhold, will you be doing a pioneering job or is there actual business in your territory? Do any of your present accounts buy?

3. Is there a big enough market for the product in your territory without the house accounts?

4. Will the principal allow you to sell a competitive line into the "house account"? Of course, the answer will be an emphatic "No!" But if the theme is pressed, you will often hear, "We will turn these house accounts over to you when we see what you can do."

After you have represented the principal for a short time and have brought in some good requests and orders, try to set a minimum. "How much do I have to do to handle GCE, the biggest account around?"

It will usually turn out to be, "How long do I have to represent you before I can handle GCE?"

GCE may be the pet account of the firm's founder. There are firms who regard these first large accounts with almost superstitious awe on the premise that "Dad always said we'd go out of business if we lost GCE."

After you have proven yourself, the firm may still want the account handled centrally even though it will pay you commission for everything going into your territory.

5. If you do decide to handle the product, or line, subject to "house account" disabilities, make sure you have an agreement with the principal that you will do absolutely nothing at these accounts even though you sell them other products. If you don't, you will soon find "emergencies" arising, telephone calls asking you to "please handle this just once," being asked to pick up emergency shipments, or even to pass messages on to the buyer.

Stick to your agreement of "no handling," or you will find yourself an unpaid messenger who has lost status with both principal and account. The buyers will say: "I didn't know you handled the PTL line. You mean they won't allow you to sell me?"

The principal will soon be saying, "Get R. H. to do it. . . . R. H. is right there. . . . Sure they will . . . R. H. is afraid of losing our line."

In these cases it is better to be hard-nosed than an accommodating patsy who has become known as "our messenger" to the largest accounts.

After a two-year period of successful representation, most reps are given commission for everything coming into their territory from house accounts.

PIONEERING—THE WHOLE TROUBLED AREA

How and Why Pioneering Costs Are Shared by the Principal

"Pioneering" usually means the merchandising of a new company rather than the sale of a new product or line.

If a "new product" is one whose advantages can immediately be seen:

1. In the consumer field where its novelty and use will make it an obvious seller,

2. In the industrial field where its cost-saving effectiveness or its new value-producing qualities are readily apparent,

this is not pioneering; it is merchandising.

Pioneering consists of:

1. Taking a highly competitive product—or line—into a new market. The product is made by a company which is not known as a supplier to that market.

2. Taking a high-priced capital product into a market where the savings or virtues of the product are not readily appreciated by one and all.

We will talk about the high-priced machine later. It represents a special type of effort.

But how do you justify taking on the first example, the highly competitive product in a new market made by a company which is not well known—or which is even unknown—in your territory?

Principal evidently wants to open your market, otherwise he wouldn't be entertaining the thought or advertising for someone.

Suppose a large sales agency is selected on a strictly commission basis. The agency won't be able to give the principal much attention. It can't afford to. A large agency's overhead compels it to concentrate on products which sell fast. It rarely has enough margin to pioneer anything which will take too long to put over.

The manufacturer feels he needs a small or middle-size agency so that he can get the attention his product "deserves."

Say you fall into that class.

You have investigated the principal's facilities. Don't ever take them for granted. There is hardly an agent around who hasn't been caught at some time or other by a manufacturer's brilliant word picture of "my great plant." It may be only a dream of the future.

But this principal's assertions have been checked out.

He does have a good working plant.

He does have financial backing; or his credit rating is good.

He gives excellent value . . . but no one in your particular market knows it.

From what you know of your territory, it will take about a year to get the product started, plus a lot of hard running on your part.

The product, or line of products, has definite potential, but you could also be spending your time running around and selling products which have immediate cash income.

This is the center of the problem.

It's all very well for someone who doesn't have to pay your bills to tell you to "always take the long view." But in the beginning of every business the "long view" may hinge on the next commission check. So some reps have taken to charging a flat fee for their services; some are charging their out-of-pocket expenses.

One agent charges a flat monthly fee, of which 50 percent is refunded after a year by means of a 1 percent cut in commissions until the figure is reached. This agent has found that a manufacturer who is paying a fee to build up a territory will be doing his best to get it on an independent basis as quickly as possible.

Naturally, it is best if you can work independently, but not everyone has that kind of capital. If you don't, and some manufacturer shows you a line which has promise—but only promise—make sure you get a contract which will enable you to enjoy the fruits of your pioneering.

Then negotiate with the manufacturer so that you both share the high cost of introducing the line.

The New High-priced Line

You are offered a chance to represent this new high-priced, slow-moving line in your territory exclusively. Sometimes there is an invisible benefit under certain conditions. If you are relatively new in business, ask yourself: Will taking on this line bring me prestige and open doors for my regular lines? Is this the type of line which will take a year to sell and then go big?

Then decide by following up:

1. Is the manufacturer ready to help promote the line? This will also promote your name.

2. Will the firm furnish sample orders?

3. Will they pay for mailings?

4. Will they negotiate on the extensive expenses this will cost you?

If you can gain prestige,

If the line can be sold as part of your regular sales calls,

If it will open doors,

If it won't bankrupt you by taking up all your time,

If it is actually a line which can be sold and will go big after a year,

THEN GO AHEAD!

If you are an established representative, there is only one other question: Does it complement your line right now, or will it get in the way of what your people are promoting to their customers?

The New Machine

You are an industrial representative. You are offered a machine "years ahead of its time." The promises are terrific—if it works. The manufacturer swears on a stack of bibles that all the bugs are out, that he can make deliveries within a stated period of time, that this machine will make your fortune.

But you have been burned before.

Ask for proof.

Will the manufacturer send in a machine for testing on a ninety-day or six-month basis? There is nothing like seeing a machine working under actual day-in-and-day-out production stresses. Controlled conditions in a manufacturer's plant where everyone knows how to handle "The Monster" do not make for good testing grounds. The machine should be tested in the field.

The manufacturer agrees.

Now go to one of your accounts that can really use the machine. Tell the people frankly that you think it's a great machine but you want a definitive test. Will they do it?

If they agree, remind the P.A., the production manager, and everyone else that the best machine in the world has bugs. The best machine in an imperfect world is imperfect.

And remember that yourself. You are not interested in perfection. Cost reduction is what you are looking for.

After the test period:

1. Does your account think they might buy the machine,

"though of course we should get a discount because it is a used machine"?

2. Is it run easily after sixty days by your account's regular operators? What do they think of it? This is important.

3. Is new machining needed?

4. Has everyone at your account's plant set himself up as a critic because he knew the machine was in just for testing?

5. Are there heavy and costly maintenance problems?

6. Does it do its job at a sizable cost reduction?

7. Have some of your other accounts heard about it?

By answering these questions you now have a real selling presentation which in turn should be passed on to the manufacturer, since he financed the whole thing.

If you financed it, keep the data for yourself.

Unless you have very very good financial backing, you do not start a representative business with this type of principal.

The "Me-Too" Product

A new principal wants you to sell an off brand at a good discount . . . against his regular sales force. The product is exactly the same as what is being sold now under a well-known brand name. Your product will not have the known brand name or the promotion behind it. Price will be the main—the only—selling point.

INDUSTRIAL SELLING

This is a good deal. As long as good quality control can be assured, the purchasing agent would rather buy the product for less no matter what the name is.

SELLING FOR CONSUMER DISTRIBUTION

1. The manfuacturer is doing this because more production

is needed to reduce overhead. Branded sales aren't high enough yet.

2. Manufacturers try to develop a new name in the market before competition jumps them with lower prices.

3. It will be four or five years before this new product is in full distribution—mostly because of lack of promotion money. After that time it may possibly even beat out its higher-priced brother. When that happens, you know there's a good chance you'll be out.

4. Will it be worthwhile to do all the development work that will be necessary? Will it pay off in sales and commissions? Will the low price be able to get you into places you've never sold before?

The mere fact that an association with a principal doesn't look as though it's going to be permanent is no reason to turn it down.

Immediate benefits sometimes steer you into long-term benefits you never expected. Because of your association with this "me-too" product, you may become known as an expert in that particular field. Other manufacturers will seek you out. After all, you are in business; perhaps you will be able to develop a competitor before you are dumped because of the good job you have done.

YOU HAVE BEEN OFFERED THE LINE YOU'VE ALWAYS FOUGHT ... COMPETITIVELY

You have just been offered a line that's always been terrific competition. You've always—or usually—outsold it. But the line has always been a headache. Should you take it on?

Ask yourself: "Why is it being offered to me now?"

1. Does the manufacturer change agents frequently? ("I'm always looking for the best—and you are it" is the reason the principal gives you.)

2. Is he trying to show up competition . . . or did he give the last agent a hard time? Ask your accounts. They know.

3. How much will you lose by giving up your present principal (competition always looks like a world beater until you begin to work with it)?

4. What will your accounts think? Will they willingly switch over, or will it be a long, hard pull? Will a substantial number of buyers stick with your present principal (and their new agent) because he has done an excellent job in the past? Will you suffer on some of your other product lines because you've let competition (and a new agent) in?

5. What will be the reactions of your other principals? Will they think they'd better start looking around before you give them the heave-ho?

In other words, never change for the sake of changing—or even for that seductive 1 or 2 percent extra. You figure, "Let's see, that'll mean at least $4,000 extra!"

It will if you don't lose any sales.

When you change principals for no good "account-value" reason, you are not going to take 100 percent of your old business with you. You may end up with a net loss.

That's why you have to try and make sure that every aspect of a change is profitable before you move; and try to project that profit picture three years in advance.

PROMOTION COSTS

A manufacturer wants you to go for part of the promotion cost of a blitz by mail into your territory. The reason given is: "If you pay for part of it, we know you'll be more interested."

It's an excellent reason, too.

If you can get away with it, pay none of the cost. After all, the greatest permanent benefit and profit of any promotion piece do go to the manufacturer. However, if you can't back out, and if you do see some personal profit in the offing, stick to the rules.

If you are an industrial representative, you go for the costs of mailing *(not printing)* the piece to your present and prospective accounts *provided* all the answers come to you.

In this case you are furnishing the all-important factor: the names, as well as the postage.

If all the answers go back to the manufacturer before they come to you ("so that we can keep a permanent file"), the normal course is for him to supply the names as well as the postage.

If you are an agent in the consumer field and the promotion consists of a mailer going to charge account bills, it will be good business to go for a percentage of the cost. Not only because of the prospective business—it will enhance your prestige with the buyer and merchandise manager as "a decision maker we can do business with in a hurry."

If you are a representative in the consumer goods field, you usually go for the costs of mailing (again, not the printing costs) to distributors, jobbers, etc., as long as the answers come to you directly because your name and address are *printed* on the promotion.

PROBLEM PRINCIPALS

"One of my principals is out of this world when it comes to problems. When do you think about dropping a principal?"

If it's only what you think of as inefficiency in getting out certain orders, etc., that can happen with anyone. In fact, it may mean that the principal's products are so excellent that Quality Control is slowing things up. Delivery problems, late estimates, "favored customers" who aren't yours—these are all problems that can be ironed out in personal meetings.

However, if a principal

1. Consistently underpays you,

2. Makes each commission statement the basis for long arguments,

3. Hides shipment notices so that you hear about them only from your accounts,

4. Does not send you copies of acknowledgments at the same time they go to customers,

5. Is always finding means of clipping 1 percent from you,

6. Is consistently late with your money,

7. Seems to resent the fact that he has to pay you any commissions at all,

8. Does not inform you of orders which have come in from your territory directly,

These are undesirable attributes. Don't hang on. Try to change as quickly as possible. You have enough exasperation as it is.

When you do drop this manufacturer, let your accounts, and your other principals, know why—if possible, with documented proof.

RETURNS: NOTHING—AND NOBODY—IS PERFECT

A manufacturer feels that the product wasn't sold right, which is why one of your accounts is returning it. They want you to pay for part of the costs.

1. If the product was sold according to specs and the principal didn't meet those specs, tell them so (see letter No. 1) politely. They are annoyed about having to do an expensive job over again and want to take it out on anybody around. You happened to be the first one who came to mind.

2. If the parts come up to published specs, it means your account's engineering department fouled up and you are being used for cover. However, it is a key account. Tell the story to your principal. Affirm that you are going to get blood on the next order. Point out that there is no reason for you to pay. This is a cost of doing business. (See letter No. 2.)

3. It's a consumer product and the colors didn't meet the descriptions. It's still the manufacturer's trouble.

4. You did not sell it right. Acknowledge your error. Everyone is human. Tell your principal you did it. You'll both have a better relation from here on in. (Letter No. 3.)

LETTER NO. 1

The product was sold according to specifications

Dear Ms. Salazar:

    I have gone over the disputed sale to GCE (P.O. 6-79015. Our Job 61098) where they are returning the ratchets for reworking. According to their spec., with which we all concurred, the ID was to be 7.017" with tolerances 1/64". Our factory did not meet those specs in any way.

    As I am sure you will be the first to agree: a part that is made out of tolerance, and not to spec., and cannot be reworked by the account's own shop (GCE tried before they decided to send the ratchets back) has to be made good by the manufacturer. I know you wouldn't want it any other way.

    If we had sold this job verbally, without blueprints furnished to you, I would certainly be sympathetic to your claim. However, in this case we supplied all necessary blueprints when we requested quotation and again when we transmitted the order. They were exactly the same in both cases.

    Therefore, we did sell the order in question correctly.

                          Sincerely,

LETTER NO. 2

The key account's engineering (or purchasing) department fouled up. You are going to cover for them

Dear Ms. Salazar:

    You and the factory are absolutely right. We all did our job right, but GCE's people

fouled up. They are asking that we "take" this
one. They'll see to it that we don't lose out
in the very short run.

As you know, every now and then the engineering and purchasing people get all fouled
up because the lines of communication aren't
very clear. That's what happened here.

Stanton, the P.A., asked that we "take
this one" (even though he knows we were right),
and he'll be grateful. When someone like Stanton
tells me that, it's money in the bank.

If you'll just look upon this as advertising, or a cost of doing business, I'm sure
that in the very near future you'll get back
more than double whatever the cost of rework-
ing those ratchets to the "correct" size will
come to.

Sincerely,

LETTER NO. 3
You fouled up

Dear Ms. Salazar:

You are absolutely right. I fouled up
selling that GCE P.O. 9-67165, our Jacket
34765.

No excuses.

Well, we all make mistakes, and I shall
certainly have to forego my commission on
this order in order to help pay for the error.

Yours,

NOTES: Don't say you'll be "happy" to forego your commission.
You won't.

Make the letter short and to the point.

Never give an excuse or an apology. Later, when the whole
thing has blown over, treat it like a comedy. The bad effects will
be blown away in the laughter.

ARE FACTORY VISITS A WASTE OF TIME?

Yes—if all you are going to do is sightsee.

Make them profitable by enlarging your human contacts among the people who help get out your work. You spend more time writing and talking to your plant contacts, fighting with them, and cajoling them than you do with any single key account. Plant visits can cut down your fighting time and get more work done for you.

You know the sales manager and the assistants. They are on your side because they have to be. Without sales, where are they?

Make sure you get to know the secretaries so that you aren't just a voice on the telephone to them. Secretaries, as you must know, can smooth your way to fast quotations. They know who to talk to in the factory when you need something done. A secretary on your side can be worth five telephone calls to some scheduling assistant who regards your order as just one more headache.

Get to know the estimators. What do they look for? What are their troubles? A lunch or a drink with an estimator can give you the feel of what's going on better than all the rah-rah bulletins your manufacturer's promotion people get out. Remember that estimators are the ones who are caught between production and sales with the treasurer making nasty side remarks. If the estimators are on your side, they may be able to suggest some slight change in the request which will give you the 5 or 8 percent differential which means orders.

Production! Everyone is always slamming the production department (or so they tell you). Be different. Tell production how wonderful they are, no matter what your private reservations may be. The sales rep who praises them once in a while is liable to become one of their heroes. It all helps when you're trying to get shipments out in a hurry.

Say hello to traffic. Let them know what a good job they do for you. Traffic can find faster, more economical ways to make your shipments. If you have to do a tracing job (it happens to everyone), they can make the long, time-consuming job much shorter.

Lastly, or perhaps even first, get to know the treasurer's people—the ones who figure your commissions, who get out the right billings, who get the checks out, who can see that credits are sent promptly. Let them tell you their troubles—they have them by the gross. At the same time they'll be letting you know how your troubles with them can be fixed.

You will never have a trouble-free relation with any of your principals; that just is not human nature. But you can get the odds in your favor by treating the people at your sources the way you treat the people at your accounts—listening to their troubles courteously and then getting what you want done.

In this case it's the equivalent of getting the order.

COMPLIMENTS

Everyone in the world likes compliments—especially production people. They get hit on the head from all quarters, at all times. So when you can go out of your way to make them feel good, do it. You'll find that a memo like the one written below will be put up on the company bulletin board and you'll be classed as one-of-the-people-we-do-things-for-around-here.

Don't do it promiscuously. But when something happens that really deserves a compliment, tell them. Production people take pride in their work, too.

```
FROM:  You

TO:    Mr. J. Raschlin, Production

Dear Joe:

        I have just had a terrific compliment
paid me which really belongs to you. GCE
told me that their last four shipments have
not only been on time; everything sailed
through their quality inspection without a
hitch. Joe, I bitch enough when there's trou-
ble, so I want you to know how pleased every-
```

one at GCE is. As J. S. Hart, the Senior
P.A., said, "Keep up the good work."
    Please thank everyone involved for GCE
and me personally.

                                        Yours,

CC: Sales Manager
    Quality Control

LOVE THOSE TRAFFIC PEOPLE!

Shipping clerks can make your life a lot easier if you treat them as important people. Too many reps are apt to think of them as machines.

They aren't.

Write notes to them directly (copy to sales manager at all times) explaining your requests. Remember, there are times when there are priorities in packing and shipping. If you are known as the "wise guy," your shipments are liable to go last.

Even if it's a small shipping department, always give the shipping clerk a title.

FROM: You   DATE.......

TO: Head of Traffic   Re: GCE Shipments

Dear Chris:

GCE wants all their shipments from us to go via
Zamperville Trucking. Now, Chris, I know you
don't like Zamperville and you feel you get
better service when you use Ripley. Most likely
you're right, because you know traffic. But,
Chris, GCE specifies Zamperville, and if we
ship by them and something goes wrong, we're
home free. But if it goes via Ripley and we're
one day late, they'll run us through the grind-
er. So, Chris, I'm afraid we'll have to go
along with them.

                                        You

TROUBLE—GET IT FIXED FAST!

But when there's trouble—or even the smell of future trouble—have no compunction about putting it right on the line.

```
Memo:

FROM:  You                      DATE:

TO:    Sales Manager            RE: Trouble at GCE
       Production
       Quality Control
       Traffic

       GCE has rejected twelve ratchets on the last
shipment for reasons attached and are sending
them back for reworking.
       Perhaps these were damaged in transit, in
which case I'd advise checking the packaging.
       Otherwise, please have QC bear down on the
next shipments to GCE. Too many rejects will
land us on the doubtful list, and this is too
good an account to lose for a reason like Quality
Control.
```

ON THE SALES MANAGER'S COPY, IN RED INK: TOM: H E L P !

GET THE CORRECT COMMISSION

There are reps who hate to write when their commissions aren't right. They feel cheap "bothering the plant just because someone made a few errors." There is no reason to feel so. If you change a price from a written quotation even slightly, you'll soon have to give the plant a full explanation.

Don't write the sales manager about any insufficiencies in your statement. The note is liable to lie around on his desk for a week. *Send him a copy.*

```
FROM:   You                      DATE
TO:     Miss Rogers, Acctg Dept  Re: Commission on
                                     Job 73271
Dear Miss Rogers:
        I note that commission on the above order
seems to have been cut 2% without explanation.
Please let me know why.
CC: J. L. Dranow, Sales Manager
```

Never let a wrong commission slip by. Calling attention to it shows the plant that you're on the ball. "He catches everything" is what they'll say about you. You'll get more respect.

CHAPTER FOUR

How letters help you get and keep key accounts

There is no substitute for personal calls. If you think you can get and keep key accounts by writing letters and making telephone calls, forget it.

But personal business letters will confirm and reinforce good impressions. They will emphasize the points you made in your verbal presentation and focus them sharply when it counts. They will help you get over rough spots.

Letters can be used by the buyer to prove to management that you are a good supplier or a good potential supplier. Letters, memos, and brochures can be your stand-in when someone who is trying to undermine your position says, "How do you know they can do it to our specs?" With your letter file in hand, the buyer is in a position to prove what you can do—or have done. He has it in writing.

If an important job is in the offing and production, at a management meeting, says, "How d'you *know* it'll be here on time?" the buyer can pull out your letter or memo and say, "Here's the confirmation." That statement stands up a lot better than "They gave me the date over the phone."

Management wants to see something like that in black and white. The heads want something solid they can put into the program. It's not a question of ducking responsibility. After all, when you are running production lines at $10,000 to $50,-000 an hour, or a department store, or a chain, where just the real estate goes into the millions, you want—and are going to get!—something better than "I think they can do it" or "They say they might deliver on time." You are going to demand documented proof.

Now a word about the letters which follow:

They are all written for competitive situations. Even if your product is so unique your trade must buy it, remember that someday, and soon, competition will loom on the horizon. If you have established friendly, helpful relations with your accounts, you'll be able to meet it with a minimum of trouble.

Letters are a necessary adjunct to good relations with your accounts. But they *must* always say something. In most cases they are an absolute necessity. Where they aren't, they should not be written. In that case they are a waste of time to your account and yourself.

It must be stressed that these letters are models—and only models. Everything but the most routine acknowledgments should have your own touch. Selling is such a personal, unhackneyed way of life that only people who can inject themselves into face-to-face selling, letter writing, and phone calls make a success.

"Injecting yourself" means being yourself. It is a truism that a sincere SOB will do a better job than an SOB covered with a sweet william veneer. Therefore, each letter should have "you" in it.

The letters begin with forms of presentation which are made under varying circumstances. There are also examples of confirmations, acknowledgments, letters explaining production delays, letters acknowledging criticisms, etc.

Again, they are not the last word. They won't be until "you" are in them. That is why it is a good idea to keep a file called "Successful Letters." Refer to it when you're in a jam. It'll help you collect your thoughts and make them more meaningful.

Every time a buyer signs his name to an order, he is putting himself on the line. Therefore, every time you sign a letter, you are letting the purchasing agent and the key account know that you are right on the line with them.

You have something unique in your field. You know it isn't going to remain unique for very long. Your job is to get as many interviews and sales as possible.

This is a general letter to the best accounts you are not selling. You know the buyer's name in each case because, if the account is worthwhile, you have taken the time to find out.

Always enclose two brochures: one for the buyer, one for the department which will use your product.

Clip your card to each brochure.

```
Dear Mr. Roberts:

Barbell's new CROSS HATCHING DEVELOPER has just
been introduced.

What does it mean to you?

        SAVINGS: How much will the cost of wil-
                 tons drop when you consider
                 that the new CROSS HATCHING
                 DEVELOPER will definitely save
                 17% in production time?

        PROFITS: The new CROSS HATCHING DEVEL-
                 OPER can work IN COLOR by mak-
                 ing one eleven-minute change-
                 over. The same machine can do
                 two jobs.

        COST:    You're going to need replace-
                 ment parts for your old cross
                 hatching developer. The cost
                 of these replacements parts
                 will pay for the new CROSS
                 HATCHING DEVELOPER.

The new Cross Hatching Developer is in produc-
tion now. The bugs are out—it took us three
years of continual running under factory condi-
tions to find them. We did it. You won't have
to.

Since I will be in Hillsdale next week, I'd like
to show you more than even these brochures can.

I will call Tuesday to arrange a convenient
time.

                          Yours truly,
```

When you are writing to a key account for an interview, write about one item which you know will capture the buyer's attention. One hot item (or service) which the buyer must use—and on which you have something new to offer—will capture interest a lot faster than a general letter which only tells about the fine outfit you represent. They are already doing business with fine outfits.

Why should they see you?

Dear Ms. Wraither:

Barbells, Inc., has developed a faster and more accurate method of manufacturing the JBF baseboards used in the assembling of radios.

The quality you may judge for yourself in the enclosed samples.

Delivery to your specifications can now be accomplished in one-half the lead time you ordinarily have to allot to this part. This means less inventory—and less investment in inventory—for your company. It also means that during changeovers you won't have so many write-offs.

I shall be in Daresville next week. May I call upon you to explain this new departure in baseboard manufacture?

Yours truly,

You are a new firm in the supply field. Your established competition regularly sends out bulletins and sales letters offering cut prices. You have zeroed in on the names of fifty big accounts; their credit is good and they are within profitable daily delivery range.

You know their greatest need is fast service.

You feature price on one or two items to pay the buyer for seeing you. Fast delivery is going to keep him doing business with you.

How do you offer it?

> Dear Mr. Eldridge:
>
> We are a new firm in the supply field, with new ideas, spanking new stock, enthusiastic people. Most of all, we have a real conception of old-fashioned courtesy and devotion to quality.
>
> Our two principals have thirty years of combined knowledge of what the offset printing field needs and have set up this business to prove it. They know you need fast delivery; we have our own truck for "got to have it NOW" supplies.
>
> Credit? D&B will give you the bare facts about us.
>
> I'd like to fill in the rest and show you how you can save time and money doing business with us.
>
>> For openers, we offer four-color plate resolvers for the same price you are paying for two colors.
>>
>> Three hundred wipers at $1.79/C.
>>
>> Delivery WHEN YOU NEED IT.
>
> We're anxious to please you and we have the backing to do it.
>
> I'll be calling you on Wednesday for that appointment, and I'll come with or without my order pad. Just let me know.
>
>> Yours truly,

The purchasing agent has answered an ad. The inquiry has been sent along to you for action.

First of all, you should take it for granted that it was done because someone in the relevant department said, "Say, this might be for us. Why not find out about it?" Always send along two brochures or two spec sheets: one for the purchasing agent's file and one for the department which will be the final user of the material.

It is much easier then for the department head to call purchasing and say, "Why don't we try some of their 4392 AX?" The buyer doesn't have to ask him what it's all about; purchasing's own copy of your offering is ready at hand.

Dear Mrs. Nostrand:

Thanks for answering our ad in the_____.
I am enclosing two brochures on the new marking devices we have just introduced.

Barbells, Inc., offers several services which
we do not advertise—services which have proven
they will save breakdown time on your marking
equipment.

As I will be in your neighborhood next week,
I'll call and set up an appointment at your
convenience.

Yours truly,

The list of parts you stock is so varied it is impossible for you to know exactly what is needed "now" by a key account. You cannot use the "unique" approach.

Therefore it is necessary for you to use two hooks or attention-getters in your letter: service and price. By trying for a contract, you can become one of the key account's regular suppliers, which is your true aim.

This letter is in answer to a mailing or an ad. It can also be slightly changed for general use, as shown in the next letter.

The time and effort spent in getting the specific buyer's name will pay for itself in the very short run!

Dear Ms. Chesley:

We're happy to send along information about our supply service.

Please note that the prices shown are good for six months ending December 31st. In these days of rocketing prices we could almost call them permanent! In fact, for people who take a year's contract to buy a minimum of $500, the prices do remain stable for one year, with the proviso that if they go down, you get the benefit of the reduction. If they go up—we gulp and bear it.

There are other areas of our service I'd like to explain to you. We are continually in your area; therefore, I'll call on Tuesday and we can set up a convenient date.

Now for a variation on the theme. This is the same letter slightly altered for general purposes.

The specific buyer's name is still necessary. How much serious attention do you generally pay to "Occupant" letters you get?

Dear Ms. Chesley:

Attached you'll find a list of parts most used in factories. We carry every one of them, plus lots of odd balls you won't find anywhere else.

Please note that the prices shown are good for six months ending December 31st. In these days of rocketing prices we could almost call them permanent! In fact, for people who take a year's contract to buy a minimum of $500, the prices do remain stable for a year, with the proviso that if they go down, you get the benefit of the re-duction. If they go up—we gulp and bear it.

Just drop a line on this note; mail in the self-addressed envelope, and I'll be glad to stop by at your convenience.

Big-ticket items—capital-expenditure machinery—are usually first inquired about by engineering or production people. They are the ones who can usually spot a cost reduction from afar.

You write to the engineer with a copy (so noted in your letter) to the purchasing agent. In this way he will be alerted to the engineer's request.

Sometimes salesreps think they can bypass purchasing. Once in a while the idea is successful, too. But most of the time it results in the purchasing agent scouring the field for competition which will do "everything your machine can do . . . at a lower price."

Your hoped-for short cut merely means you have to work that much harder to get the purchasing agent's signature on the purchase order.

```
Dear Mr. Jonathan:

Thanks for asking about our New Barbell Three-
Ring Cross Hatcher. You, as an engineer, can
immediately appreciate the value of the three
rings to the cross-hatching process. It not
only saves time but it will reduce the number
of rejects almost 45%.

Your purchasing people will be pleased to hear
about the cost reduction it can make in your
production. Therefore, I am sending a copy of
this letter and a brochure to Mr. L. E. Jones.

It would open everyone's eyes to see the Three-
Ring Cross Hatcher in operation under actual
factory conditions. We'll be glad to bring it
around to your plant and set it right to work
on your own products.

As the man says, your company will be under no
obligation.

I'll give you a ring next week with a view to
setting up a convenient date.
```

You make, distribute, or represent a line of consumable items which can be used generally.

Someone from production, the warehouse, or material handling has stopped by your booth at a show. In your letter to the inquirer you should stress the one product which responds to the particular need for which information was requested. A specialist is not interested in the broad spectrum of products a purchasing agent has to monitor.

A copy to purchasing is necessary to break the inertia which says, "Why change?"

It's not that a buyer is "married" to any particular supplier. Many times it's just habit that makes them feel (and say), "Why call new people in? I'm sure Joe Jones Co., our usual supplier, can do just as well."

The "particular product" appeal can overcome habit.

```
Dear Ms. Williams:

I want to thank you for taking the time to
visit with us at the NEIA show.

As you may have guessed, we exhibit only our
general lines at these shows. We did not have
on hand our 395 XR, which is specially de-
signed to handle the production and movement
of barbells.

If it is convenient, I'd like to get together
with you and your purchasing people next week.
The proven cost reduction the 395 XR can show
you will be of real interest.

I'll call Tuesday for an appointment.
```

You have been selling one division of GCE for a significant period. Now it is time to make a call on another division.

Properly handled, this should not be classed as a cold call.

A letter will give the buyer a chance to contact his colleague in the other division and ask, "Who is he?"

Always ask permission from the buyer whose name you are going to use.

Dear Mrs. Metcalf:

We have been doing business with Mr. J. C. Ryan of the Rototail division of Barbells, Inc., for the past year and a half. While we haven't captured every quotation sent us during that time, we have priced and delivered enough JCA1 handles to make us a significant supplier.

Our plant now has equipment which can profitably be used by the JAS division. Our engineers have come up with a new design which, we believe, will halve the time of manufacture of banding nuts.

The savings you will be able to show in this part alone should make for significant cost reductions throughout the plant.

Since I will be out your way next week, I'll call and we can set up an appointment.

In selling heavy-ticket machinery or processes, you should know costs as well as your customer does. In any highly competitive field, your estimates should be within 5%.

Dear Mr. Wesley:

Some of the most profit-minded companies in the field have been inquiring about the new Cross Wing Hatcher we've just introduced. We think it is going to revolutionize the industry.

I know that your company will want to give a lot of thought to this new concept of manufacturing from both a profit and a service viewpoint.

   1. We can prove it will reduce the time of manufacture by 22%.

   2. We can prove it will reduce your rejects by more than 31%.

   3. We can prove you don't need a Ph.D. in Nuclear Physics to run it. An ordinarily intelligent worker will make it sing within a week.

I have enclosed three brochures so that the proper people in Barbells, Inc., can study them at their leisure.

I'll be in Carlsberg in two weeks' time. I am sure you will want to know even more about the new Cross Wing Hatcher at that time.

This is not a key accounts letter. It's for initiating sales by mail of small-ticket items.

There are some products which can be used by factories of all types. They do not give anyone a competitive edge nor are they high-priced. They are used in such small volume that it does not pay to travel with them.

However, in overall sales these products can represent a steady, moderate sales volume.

You have decided to sell a product like this by mail. Therefore you get a list of buyers' names and go ahead.

There may be a few plants you know will be able to use a sizable volume of this product; or you may just want to get into a certain plant. In that case you end your letter by asking for an appointment.

But for the usual small-volume plant, you may decide to use the ending shown.

Dear Ms. Hopkins:

Enclosed you will find samples of ID Tabs, which are used for quickly sorting out the multiple shipments which have always caused such expensive errors and irritating delays in the traffic department.

These tabs have been tested in factories all over the United States for the past two years. In plant after plant they have cut down sorting errors and wrong shipments. And all at an average cost of $150 per year! There is no labor cost, since they are attached at the time of packaging.

The material used is Mylar, and the adhesive is guaranteed to be permanent. We stock the tabs in twenty different colors—ten prime colors and ten with black bars.

We will be glad to send you a trial assortment of tabs for $20 which will enable your people to make four hundred error-free shipments. The savings in out-of-pocket expenses, to say nothing of customer irritation, will more than pay for

the trial. After that we know you'll become a
regular user.

Just attach the enclosed coupon to your letterhead and send it to us. We'll bill you. If you
don't like the tabs, just send whatever you have
left back and we'll forget the whole thing.

Yours truly,

You have been recommended to an account by one of his suppliers. Even though your contact is going to telephone the buyer, it is a good idea to get a letter off first for an entirely different reason. The purchasing agent is just liable to look upon the recommendation as a chance for the supplier to get information he wouldn't get otherwise. Therefore, it is wise to stress the security angle in this case.

In fact, anytime you use competition as a reference in your general letters to an industry, it is well to stress security.

It is also a very good idea to ask your good customer whether he minds your soliciting the rest of the industry.

Dear Mr. Hoyt:

Mr. Justin Barnard, Jr., production manager of Robbins, Inc., has suggested that I show you our new hatching process. He feels it would do a good job on your semi-detached barbell line.

As you will note from our letterhead, we have been in the business for the last fifteen years and have shown an excellent growth pattern in that time. We've been able to do it because we can gear our production line to yours. We also have a "zero defects" program that is tied into our production people's bonus.

But that's only on the production end. We can guarantee you complete security in your dealings with us. Our feeling is this: You can tell competition, or anyone else, whatever you wish about your business. They'll never hear about it from us.

I would like to show you how our interests coincide. Since I will be out your way next week, I'll telephone and set up a convenient appointment.

Yours truly,

You have received a request for quotation from a purchasing agent. You do not make, or represent a manufacturer of, the item they need. If the company is a large one, you'll take time out to tell them so. But will you do so if it is a small company?

You never know what is going to happen in the future. Small firms can suddenly become big users of your products. Sometimes they are bought out and you find yourself talking to a purchasing agent who remembers that "they wouldn't even quote me when we were a small outfit."

Therefore, it is always a good idea to answer every inquiry no matter how small the outfit.

Dear Mrs. Sakale:

I am sorry to report that we do not manufacture Cross Grain Barbells as requested in your inquiry 71-12.

Our work for companies in your field covers a wide area of barbell manufacture, including pitched, outranged, and the new hatched types.

Enclosed you will find both your request for quotation, our current catalog, and samples of work we have done recently in the barbell field. If you need any further information on anything we make, please get in touch with me.

I hope you will try us again in the areas where, in view of our long-time relationship with customers, we excel.

Yours truly,

Sometimes you are asked to make an emergency run to meet a special situation. You find you can do it. Of course, you'll telephone at once. But get it in writing, too.

Buyers are rotated every so often.

Perhaps an entirely new buyer will take over in thirty days. Naturally, you want the new buyer to know your past record. He will, if you have taken the trouble to write. He'll find it in the letter file, or clipped to the order. You won't have to sell yourself over and over again.

It will also be a means of beating out competition which does not have a letter file of past accomplishments for the buyer to read.

It's a case of "these people have done a lot of favors for us in the past." The new buyer is going to need favors, too, especially when production starts yelling for those parts NOW. Who better to keep on good terms with than you?

And all because of your letters.

```
Dear Ms. Paul:

As I told you over the phone today, my produc-
tion people have been able to schedule the four
hundred hatchers you need.

Delivery will be made on June 23d. The extra day
is necessary to get them through quality control.

Glad we could do it for you.

Yours truly,
```

You are confirming a telephone appointment with an out-of-town buyer you have never met.

Your letterhead in his hand gives him a concrete image of you before you even step through the door. You are not so much of a stranger.

The buyer will also have your telephone number handy in case he has to cancel. He may even want you to bring along detailed information on something else which has just come up.

Your letter makes it easy for him to contact you.

Dear Mr. Cornelius:

Thanks for setting up an interview for Tuesday, March 19th, at 10:30.

I'll be bringing along the Barbell Regrinder we talked about so that it can be tested under actual field conditions. It occurs to me you may also want to look at the new Cross Hatcher, so I'm bringing one of those, too. As the man says, "no obligation" either way.

Yours,

You have had your first interview with the buyer of a key account. The firm wants further technical information about some particular item.

If the information is about price in any form, the information goes to the buyer alone.

If it is about the product, or a specification change, it is best to make several copies of the change and send them along with your letter. In that way the buyer can send along the changes to the final users while retaining a copy for purchasing alone.

The buyer should receive your letter within one week after your interview. Three days is best. After one week you will have faded from a buyer's mind.

Timing is of the essence in sales as well as in sports and life.

```
Dear Ms. Rosten:

Here is the information on the Changer speci-
fications you asked about during our meeting
on Tuesday.

I have had everything you asked for spelled
out on the attached sheet. In essence you will
find that our Cross Hatcher will enable you to
eliminate one station on your line. Therefore,
while the cost is 4% higher than your present
hatching device, the cost saved on the produc-
tion line and in inspection time should give
you a net cost reduction of 7%.

Then, too, there is the valuable plus of no
breakdown time. Barbells maintains a continual
inventory of cross hatchings which are avail-
able to you within one hour of a telephone
call.

Thanks for our interview. I am sure Barbells
can offer you the delivery and quality you
need for fast, profitable production. . .
and at a price you want to pay.

Yours truly,
```

You have a fast request from a key account you've been trying to penetrate. You know it's a fill-in—that the regular supplier must have had a breakdown.

On the other hand, it's your busy season, too, and all your machines are scheduled in depth for ninety days.

In order to meet this request, you will have to schedule overtime. Tell this to the buyer and show what your prices would be if you had the normal lead time. This lets him know that you are not taking him over the barrel while you have the chance.

Your honesty may also make him sit up and take notice.

Dear Mr. Jensen:

Attached you will find our quote on requirements listed under Reference 247AX3.

Our entire production is scheduled for the next ninety days for both shifts. In order to keep our firm commitments to our valued customers, we would have to produce your requirements on overtime and Sunday time. Premium price for labor is included in the present quotation.

If this was a regularly scheduled order with normal lead time, our price per M would have been $____ .

Thanks for allowing us to quote. Should we receive your order, please telephone us immediately so that we may get the fastest jump possible on meeting the required delivery date.

On the other hand, you find it is physically impossible to meet Jensen's requirements.

```
Dear Mr. Jensen:

I am sorry to report that we cannot handle your
requirements as listed under Ref. 247AX3.

Our entire production is scheduled for the next
ninety days for both shifts, including overtime.
Sunday is being given over to maintenance so
that we will be able to fill all our firm commit-
ments to our valued customers.

I feel it is best to let you know the situation
here at once so that you will be able to make
other arrangements.
```

Letters of congratulation are a purely personal choice. If you know the buyer well, you will telephone the moment the news breaks.

However, there are times when a letter can add something,

1. If it's to a buyer you see occasionally.

2. If by your letter you can suggest that you may have helped further his career.

Congratulations, Miss Jeremy:

It was good to read about your appointment to the new rank of Purchasing Agent for Barbells, Inc.

You'll remember that when the new stop brake equipment was installed last year, we hoped it would do a good job for the company and you. I think both objectives were realized.

The best of luck to you in your new assignment. Naturally, if there is ever anything we can do to make Barbells, Inc., and its Purchasing Agent grow, please call upon us.

Letter to a new buyer at a company you've had no luck with. This is a chance not to be missed. The buyer is new. He has no preconceptions. He will want to show that he can do a better job than his predecessor.

Perhaps you can help.

Dear Mr. Mathews:

Congratulations on your new assignment!

We have been doing work for some of the leading firms in your and allied fields. The attached brochure will give you some idea of the type of work we do and whom we do it for.

One thing our brochure does not explain is our Bonus for Value system. Our production team's bonus is based on zero defects in the parts we ship. That means parts you can depend on with a minimum of line breakdown and no kickback from your quality control people.

This is only one of the extras I would like to discuss with you in your campaign to make 'em sit up and take notice.

I'll call Tuesday for an appointment.

Letter to a purchasing agent you do not know in a company with which you have been doing business for some time.

Don't take it for granted that he will find out all about you either from the files or from the P.A. being relieved. Send a letter to precede your call. That means he or she will, at least, glance at your file before you come in.

If you have no quotes open, etc., find some good reason to call within a week.

Dear Mr. Rodriguez:

Congratulations on your new assignment!

We have been doing business with Barbells, Inc., for the past seven years and hope to continue serving you. Your predecessor, Ms. Roberts, used to say of us, "There's one outfit I never have to worry about." That, we think, is the best compliment any supplier can get.

Naturally, you're surrounded by a sea of papers at the moment, so I won't add to them. We do have two quotes open, which I'll bring over inside the week. In that way I may be of help in clearing some of them away.

If you need any immediate information, please call upon me.

Intelligent reps sell for the future! They get to know everyone in purchasing, including the clerks and assistants.

You never know when someone is going to be promoted—someone who will be buying your categories.

Therefore, when an assistant is promoted, call and send a letter of congratulations. Not only is it good manners . . .

It's also good business!

Dear Mr. Moreno:

Welcome to the status of full Buyer!

As someone keeps saying, "If you've got it, flaunt it!" You've got it, and they saw it.

The best of luck to you. Everyone knows you have the courage and the brains. All you need now is a little luck, and everyone who has ever dealt with you will see that you get it.

Sincerely,

The acknowledgment of a stock-item order or any order for something not out of the ordinary should preferably be sent on a postcard. This tends to show that good delivery and good customer care are routine with your firm.

```
Your Order .......... Requested ........
for ...............
will be delivered ................
via ............
Our Job No. is ............

Yours truly,

Barbells, Inc.
```

A complicated order should be acknowledged with every detail spelled out. If there are going to be any misunderstandings or misconceptions, get them ironed out *before* you start production.

Dear Ms. Rogers:

We want to thank you for your order P-7581, which we have entered upon our books as follows:

```
100,000 Castile Mobile Renders.
        Size: 1 3/4 X 7 3/8" (finished)
        Stock: Matte Gold Foil as per
               sample attached to this
               letter.
        Colors: MT-23 Blue
                Q-7    Red
                JVR    Yellow.
        Equipment: 7/8" Punch
                   12" gold lame string
                   looped..$12.73 per M
```

There will be a one-time nonrecurring charge of $198.70 for plates and dies.

The Castiles will be delivered within six weeks after the okay of proofs and setups.

The above order is taken subject to our usual terms of Net 30, FOB our Cartsville plant.

Thank you again for entrusting us with this fine order. We know the final product will meet with everyone's satisfaction.

Yours truly,

You are going to be seventy-two hours late with a production item.

Let the buyer know this by postcard. Seventy-two hours is usually not fatal, nor will it usually close the line down. Most plants allow some time for delay in their production schedules, since we are all human and anything can happen.

However, your postcard will forestall the hurried telephone call from a buyer who is being pushed by the production people. It will enable him to show them that he is on top of the situation at all times.

Do not send a seventy-two hour delay notice if you are going to be later. This destroys your credibility.

```
Dear Sir:

Your order...... Our Production No.......
will be delayed........

due to.....

Yours truly,

Barbells, Inc.
```

You are going to be a week late.

The time element demands a personal letter. Anything longer than a week deserves and should get a personal call *and* a letter.

But be honest. A trumped-up excuse usually smells. Not only that, but you are liable to forget what you told the buyer. Then one day at lunch you tell the story about the time four or five months ago "when the factory was in a mess" with a jammed-up schedule and two machines which collapsed at the same time.

The buyer will remember if you said something else. Your credibility will descend to a new low for the future.

Dear Mrs. Johns:

Because of an unfortunate freight tie-up which prevented the delivery of certain vital parts, we will not be able to make our shipping commitment for April 16.

We are working overtime shifts to get everything in order, and we confidently expect to make shipment on your P-7681 no later than the 23d.

Yours truly,

The way a complaint is handled spells out the entire future course of your relationship with your customer.

Even if the complaint is handled well, the relationship can still be soured by one of those sulky letters which places the whole blame on the customer's receiving or inspection department.

Take the blame cheerfully. You'll have to take it anyway, so why not do it with good grace?

This letter sells the company while it answers the complaint.

Dear Mr. Walden:

This acknowledges with thanks receipt of your letter of June 3d.

Even though your letter and the sample you sent come under the heading of "Bad News," we welcome receiving it. We take great pride in the quality of our workmanship, and when our plant does slip, it helps everyone in sales and production to know about it so we can take every step possible to correct any breakdown in our inspection procedures.

Naturally we will replace the parts at once.

I am sending your letter and a copy of this letter to our vice president in charge of manufacture. He will write you directly and advise what steps he has taken so that this cannot reoccur.

Very truly yours,

Selling to large key accounts usually means that you will be making a lot of shipments all over the country.

One day you will find dumped on your desk some small bills which have not been paid—the large ones always are.

First, check the purchase order:

1. The Purchase Order number. Did your billing clerk put in the wrong P.O. Number? She may have made a "97" become a "79."

2. Is the form or part number correct?

3. Are the "Ship to" and "Bill to" correct?

The customer's IBM will usually throw back a bill with errors in the above information.

If everything checks out okay at your end, write to the *accounts payable supervisor.* It is not necessary to know his or her name; if you do, it's a plus. A memo will do just as well as a letter. Make sure a copy of your invoice is attached. Your invoice number alone means nothing among the thousands of invoices received every day.

Accountants like all their information put before them in a neat, concise way.

MEMO

10-21-75

```
FROM:  Z. R. Winter (Sales)
       BARBELLS, INC.

TO:    ACCOUNTS PAYABLE      RE: P.O. CL 9106T
       SUPERVISOR               Invoice: G-7178
                                (Copy attached)
Gentlemen:

The above-referenced invoice has been open for
more than sixty days. If there is any reason why
it cannot be paid, please let me know.

Yours truly,
```

Usually your invoice has not been paid because someone forgot to send a receiving slip up to accounts payable.

However, there is also a chance that your shipment may have failed to pass inspection, which is always rather slow with paperwork.

One week after you have written to the accounts payable supervisor and have not received an answer, send a clean copy of your invoice to the purchasing people who initiated the order.

This can best be in memo form, too. A letter might look as if you were making a federal case out of the whole thing.

                                    11-10-75

FROM: Z. R. Winter (Sales)
      BARBELLS, INC.

TO: Mr. G. R. Senft   RE: P.O. CL 9106T

Dear Mr. Senft:

For some reason the attached invoice has not been paid.

Branch Motors tells us it was signed for by your receiving clerk on 8/10 at 2:20 P.M.

I wonder if you would be good enough to send this invoice through for payment.

Yours truly,

There is a general strike looming in your industry.

Don't take it for granted that everyone knows about it. They don't.

Information should be printed in the form of a bulletin. This tells your customer that the strike is not specifically against you. Your competition is also going to be hit.

```
The  .......... (Union)
has called a general strike against the wood,
wheel, and wagon industry scheduled to begin
at 12:00 P.M., June 21.

Industry negotiators are meeting with the
union night and day in an effort to get all
questions settled before then.
```

Some delays cannot be forecast. Everyone has wildcat strikes inflicted on them. If yours looks as though it's going to last long enough to disrupt some schedules, notify the individual buyer . . . but be optimistic.

You can't hide the news. Your competitors will be telling everyone fast enough.

Dear Ms. Roberts:

As you may know, a wildcat strike has dis-
rupted our finishing facilities. While we
confidently expect this illegal walkout to
be settled in short order, we feel you should
know the situation.

Yours truly,

TIPS ON LETTER WRITING

Winston Churchill once said that the most complicated idea can be presented on one 8 by 11 page. Your sales letter should convey the concept. Keep the technical work separate; the buyer will refer that to the engineering or production people anyway. By keeping the technical work separate, you allow purchasing to "stat" it and send it through without divulging prices and terms which may raise awkward questions before they want to answer them.

Letters to junior buyers should always be formal, especially if you are older than they are. Make sure their title is prominently displayed.

Letters to older buyers should be specific and short. They've seen it all, and many times they equate brevity with sincerity. You can compliment them by keeping your letter brief and to the point.

Every good rep knows how important secretaries are in a selling situation. If one has gone out of his or her way to help you, tell the boss. They'll both like the courtesy.

Short letters—like short sales talks—do the job best.

Use the technical language that is part of your industry's stock in trade; it makes you "one of us." But don't go out of your way to use one large word where two or three small ones will do. Simple English never needs an interpreter.

In these days of semiliterate secretaries, do not hesitate to make a minor correction in pen on the letter correcting a misspelling. It shows you read the letter before you signed it. Major corrections, of course, necessitate a new letter.

Look at your letter before you sign it. Does it say what you want it to, or will the purchasing agent have to interpret it? If he—or she—does, the odds are it will be interpreted the wrong way.

Letters to women no longer present special problems. If she signs her letters *Mrs.* or *Miss*, you follow along. But what if she signs neither? Use *Ms.*

Short letters prevent an accumulation of errors.

A sales letter must feature a "need to know." You must have something in that letter which will arouse the buyer's interest from either a personal or a company viewpoint. You may enclose brochures—but why should they be read? You may extend an invitation to send for something—why should you be answered? You may ask for an interview—why should you be let in? How well you satisfy the buyer's "need to know" will spell the degree of success your sales letter will have.

A form letter to a key account rarely gets past a secretary unless it is a "flash"—a hot offering which doesn't cost too much.

Always call—or write—with a definite idea in mind. Just as "Anything for me today?" invites a "No," so a general letter is magnetized by a wastebasket.

Write important letters first by hand. Dictating allows us to "develop our thoughts" so that they run on and on. Mark Twain once apologized for writing a long letter; he didn't have the time, he said, to write a short one. Short letters are read!

Make a virtue of necessity. If the buyer is at some distance, he may hesitate to ask you to see him. He doesn't want to be under obligation to you. Therefore, in your letters (as in your telephone calls) suggest that you are going to be in the vicinity anyway.

SUMMARY OF THE MODEL LETTERS IN THIS SECTION

1. Selling the unique—which isn't going to remain unique for long.

2. Selling the one hot item which the buyer must use.

3. You are a supply house or sell a large variety of consumable items.

4. The purchasing agent is answering your ad for consumable items.

5. You cannot use the "unique" approach.

6. Trying for a contract—general mailing.

7. Big-ticket sales—answering an engineer's inquiry.

8. Your products have a general interest—keeping the interest limited.

9. You are going after another division of a key account.

10. Big-ticket items—cold letter with estimates.

11. A product sold by mail—individually, small-volume.

12. Stressing security when you have been recommended by a supplier or another firm.

13. You do not make what the buyer is requesting.

14. You are answering an emergency today. What about tomorrow?

15. Confirming an appointment with an out-of-town buyer.

16. Letter after the first interview—the importance of timing.

17. The fill-in request from a noncustomer. You can do it at a cost.

18. You find it impossible to do but you want to keep the road open.

19. Congratulations—When to write.

20. Letter to the new buyer.

21. A new purchasing agent at the key account with whom you have been doing business.

22. A new assistant buyer is promoted.

23. The routine acknowledgment.

24. The complicated acknowledgment.

25. You are going to be seventy-two hours late.

26. You are going to be a week late.

27. Answering a complaint from a key account about quality.

28. You have not been paid: sixty days.

29. You have not been paid: ninety days.

30. A strike is threatened in your industry.

31. Notice of a wildcat strike.

CHAPTER FIVE

You have lost or are going to lose a key account

Not just an order. The purchasing agent has called you in and said, "We are not going to buy from your source any more. Nothing personal, friend; we just can't afford them."

This is the toughest situation of all in selling—especially if you had nothing to do with it. Because, hard as it is to get into a key account, once you're out, it's tougher by far to get back in. You start as a minus quantity. It will take all your patience, guts, hard work, ingenuity, and perhaps two years.

But before you do *anything*, make sure that the reason you lost this key account has been eliminated, or you stand to lost your entire business. What discourages one account will discourage all the others. And because you are the one representing the failure, your other principals will suffer, too.

Bad luck usually spreads like the plague. "That rep's people don't know what they're doing" can be your business epitaph. Stop the cause immediately, whether it's in yourself or in your plant.

We can discuss the plant's faults later—they are fairly easy to pinpoint. The hard part is to examine yourself and decide if any personal trait of yours helped to lose the account.

1. *Did you take the easy way out?* When production told you

the shipment couldn't possibly be made before the nine-teenth and your account said it had to be there by the seventeenth, did you just hope for the best and say it would be there by the seventeenth? Has this happened three or four times? Has that helped to throw out production planning's timing? Have you always blamed the delays on your principal?

2. When estimating asked, "Will GCE mind if we cut the ID by $1/64$?" did you say "Yes" before you asked the account? ("You were too busy at the time.")

3. Did you decide that, just because you'd had the account for five years now, you didn't really have to worry about it? Hell, you knew what the firm wanted . . . and when it wanted it . . . without having to run 'way up there every other week. So you stayed away. And things changed. And you didn't even know about it.

4. Did you decide, all by yourself, that GCE didn't really need that extra service you always used to give them because once you found a special shipment you had run in yourself still "hanging around the next day"? So you wouldn't take the trouble any more, and they found someone who did.

5. Because you had a "split arrangement" in effect with a principal whereby you got 50 percent of any overage above the estimate, did you "zing it to them good" two or three times because "that kid buyer will never find out she's being taken"? Then you were surprised when the "kid" not only found out but presented you with the evidence and you were out; officially because "you're 'way out of our price range."

6. Did you let success go to your head and not follow up on your promises?

7. Has the vicinity of your desk become so attractive that you can't bear to get away from it? There are lots of valid

excuses which can keep you there. "It's raining . . . or snowing," or "There's all this paperwork to get out and the girl just can't handle it," or "They like the Master's Touch on these reports. People appreciate it." But they don't help you hold your key accounts, or any other business.

8. Have you been denigrating some new agent—"Hell, he's just a kid. He doesn't know anything"? Remember, you were his age when you opened your business. "Oh, we had it tougher." Perhaps, but he is getting into your accounts now.

If none of these points honestly apply to you, then we can go on to figuring how we can get back into the key account by making sure that the causes of losing it are not operative now.

But if some of them do apply to you, take a hard look at yourself and your methods. Ask yourself, "Is this the way I would have acted when I first started this business?"

In fact, that's a good question to ask yourself at any time. Maybe you weren't so smart when you first started . . . but perhaps you made up for that in vitality, enthusiasm, sincerity, and (it's a hard word) humility.

THE PLANT HAS BEEN CARELESS BUT HAS LEARNED ITS LESSON

You have lost a key account because of stupidity or carelessness at the plant. Nothing felonious or even malicious, but the effect is the same. Because of you (*you* are always identified with your plant), the line was held up three times at the cost of $10,000 an hour.

No one is going to forgive or forget that.

How are you going to get them to?

First, you make sure that the same situation absolutely cannot exist any more. Not "perhaps"; "absolutely" is the word. Otherwise, anything you do is going to be so much wasted effort. Perhaps the loss of this account can shake the factory out of their slovenly ways. If it doesn't, get yourself another principal. This one is evidently successful in spite of himself, but the luck doesn't carry over to you.

Send this letter if the reason for the trouble has been excised.

```
Dear Mr. Raymond:

        I want you to know that I fully sympa-
thize and go along with the decision never to
let Barbells into the front door (let alone
the factory!) again.
        Any supplier who holds up the line three
times is guilty of criminal negligence.
        Barbells thinks so, too. They have fired
the scheduling manager and placed his successor
directly under production control.
        This is scant payment for the trouble you
went through, but at least it shows that Bar-
bells has caught on.

                        Sincerely yours,
```

You then stay away for three months . . . this is long enough to put a scab on the wounds.

Your first time in, you'll be greeted with: "Nothing. No. Not ever. **Nothing!**

If you are smart, you'll point out that you just dropped in to see if you couldn't be of any help. Then drop in monthly. It will take at least a year. It will even take a personal visit by the president or the production manager to convince GCE's buyers that not only has the company taken its medicine . . . it is now cured of all its former diseases.

It will take a little time after that before you start getting small orders again. Be scrupulously honest. Do not exaggerate or minimize anything. You will always be on trial from there on in.

THE PRINCIPAL SAYS HE IS RIGHT . . . HE IS WRONG

You are a rep who has lost a key account because the factory didn't come through. The principal has a president who is always right and for whom the whole world is wrong. It takes a long time for a genius to be proven right, and you don't have the time.

In a case like this, you stand to lose a key account not only for this principal but for all your others. When something goes wrong at an account again, you will be blamed; the smell of failure then extends to everything else you sell . . . and everyone else you represent.

If this erring principal will not change, cut the firm out as you would dry rot. Tell the key account immediately what you have done.

Dear Mr. Raymond:

  I want you to know that I fully sympathize and go along with your decision never to let Barbells through the front door again.

  On Tuesday I went down to Rayesville and acquainted Barbells with your decision. I also asked that we start an immediate investigation so that we could eliminate the causes of your fully justified complaints.

  In my opinion they utterly refused to do so.

  Therefore, on the same day I gave Barbells notice that I will no longer be handling their line because their service was not compatible with the service rendered by my other principals.

  Ordinarily I would have let you know this on my usual call. However, I feel so strongly about it that I felt I should communicate with you at once.

  Thank you for your consideration.

In this case you have disassociated yourself from your former principal in the interests of the rest of your line.

Make certain that you do anything in your power to help out GCE with Barbells.

Let your other principals know what you have done.

THE NEW PURCHASING AGENT IS BRINGING IN "MY OWN GROUP OF SUPPLIERS"

A new purchasing agent has been hired at your key account because of "profit-minded experience in our field." Translation: The purchasing department is about to be reorganized. Immediately the group of buyers and assistants you know and have served are either fired or transferred. Only the secretaries are left, and even they are shaken.

This new P.A. has a group of suppliers "who have proven to be trustworthy over the years. I can rely on them!" Quite possibly you may be kept on the list . . . out of politeness.

It does not matter to you why the new P.A. was brought in. It does not matter what you think of the decision. *Fall in with the thinking immediately!* They are right! Tell the new P.A. that "a reliable, economic supplier deserves a buyer's loyalty." You are in entire agreement because that's the kind of people you represent.

Thank the new P.A. for even keeping you on the list. You're going to try and prove that you are worthy of joining the select group of reliables.

Get a letter off the moment you get back to your office.

Dear Ms. Rogers:

    I want to thank you for your courtesy in explaining your personal purchasing policy.

    As soon as I got back here I went through the files for the last three years. Of the one hundred and four orders placed through us during that time, seventeen were emergencies; fifteen of these were delivered on or before the dates marked "MUST HAVE BY ... ." The other two were delivered within forty-eight hours of the re-

```
quested date. Of these I personally picked up
six orders at the airport and ran them into your
plant so that they'd be on the assembly line in
time.
      Of the one hundred and four orders, all
(except the emergencies) were supplied under
competitive quotation. We lost thirty-seven
orders during that time.
      I am not citing these figures to quote
past glory, but to show you that, on the record,
we have supplied GCE with their requirements at
good prices, on time, and, when necessary, with
that extra service which, as you so trenchantly
put it, "every customer needs now and then to
keep the line moving."
      That's why I was so delighted to know that
you rate your suppliers and their reps. We know
we'll come up high on your list.
```

THEY ARE GOING TO CENTRALIZE OR DECENTRALIZE

It is announced that the division's purchasing department is being combined outside your territory. It would not be possible to keep your contacts because of economic and other reasons.

How do you stay in?

This is why it is always smart to keep your contacts in the factory as well as in the purchasing department at good levels. Purchasing may be moving away, but production has to stay. You cannot centralize machinery. Their problems will always be here and now.

First of all, in the long haul, at a key account you can be sure that in another few years the pendulum will swing away from the way they are buying now. Then will come the announcement, "Even though we saved corporate funds buying centrally, this policy has inhibited our divisions from making those revolutionary changes our customers have come to expect from GCE. Therefore, as of May 1st, each division. . . ."

So keep up your contacts.

Every now and then stop by to see the production people. In a short while you will find that they have been authorized to buy material and jobs which cost no more than ___ dollars. If the job or material goes over the authorized level, you will find that they will issue two purchase orders so that each stays at the authorized level. Why? Because emergencies arise which cannot await chain-of-command buying. The general manager of the satellite plant which has lost production time because of it will complain bitterly to H.Q. which will then extend him this privilege. This is the first opening. This is your new foot in the door.

Getting the other foot in is done by mail . . . if the account is not being covered by another rep.

If it isn't . . . and the volume is high enough, make appointments by telephone and go up once every two or three months (according to whatever percentage of your income is covered by the amount of business you receive from them).

But no matter what happens, never drop them entirely . . . because the volume at a key account is always there. If you drop it, you'll merely be starting all over again when the plant you were formerly serving becomes a "profit center" once more.

YOU HAVE BEGUN TO PRICE YOURSELF WAY OUT OF LINE

GCE is one of those companies which keep a graph of suppliers' quotes. If you come in consistently high over a period of time, you are taken off the list and replaced by a new supplier.

You have lost four of the last four requests, and the buyer has said, "What's with you people? This is the third time you've been 'way off."

This is his way of saying, "Watch it. A few more of those and you'll be forgotten as well as gone."

What do you do?

First: Check with the estimators directly. Have rates been upped without anyone telling you?

Second: Ask, "Have we been quoting on the correct material? Or did we substitute something 'better' because we 'knew it would give the customer a better value'?"

Get the sales manager's help immediately.

```
FROM: You                DATE

TO:   J. R. S/M          RE: GCE: We're losing
                             out!

GCE is telling me we're way out of line on price
lately. What gives? We had them going beautifully
three months ago, and now we're in left field
and missing the ball consistently.

If you can give me something to tell Stanton,
the buyer, I'd sure appreciate it.

                                         You
```

You are not crying, "Wolf"; you are shaking them up.

If the price differential was caused by different material, make the report verbally, or in memo form. Do not make the report formal, or the buyer may feel you are trying to put him under the gun.

```
FROM: You                      DATE:

TO:   Mr. H. R. Stanton, Buyer  Re: Materials

Dear Harvey:

     I think I have found out why Barbells has
been coming in so high lately. Your quotes have
been asking for "best possible stock," and my
boys feel that Mylar will outperform and outlast
Acetate five or six times.
     As you know, Mylar's cost is three times
that of acetate. I have therefore asked the
plant to refigure that last quote on Acetate
to show you what the price would have been had
```

```
we quoted on it. I have also told the estima-
tors that from now on, whenever they quote on
a higher-priced stock, to also show the cost on
a lower-priced one so that you can have the com-
parison right in front of you.
```

(signed) You

In this memo you are not condemning anyone else. Your people were just being knights in shining armor. This takes the onus of high prices off you and at the same time establishes you as a value house which is trying to give something extra as well as price.

To be well motivated is all very well and good. But it does no one any good if the buyer doesn't know it.

Prices Going Up?

But suppose a memo comes back singing a familiar tune:

```
Charlie:
        Wages and material costs have escalated.
        Even the county taxes here have gone up
more than ten percent.
        But our quality remains the best, Charlie.
Our on-time service is still on time. We have
just had to raise our rates to cover costs.
        Besides, we know that everyone else in the
industry has done so, too.
        The plant is running full time, Charlie—
with two shifts. So this is the time to move in
on GCE again. You've got something to sell!
```

J. R. (the S/M)

TRANSLATION: "We're having no trouble here. The plant is going full steam ahead. What's wrong with you?

"If everyone else in the industry has raised prices, it will start showing up in your territory soon."

Sometimes there is a special situation which has been created by a new manufacturer determined to break into GCE with "home office specials." GCE's buyers will recognize this. They'll get the lower prices while they can but will still recognize the necessity of keeping alternate sources. This type of pressure takes about three to six months to let up. The new manufacturer can't keep losing money forever.

But you want to know whether or not this price rise is really an "industry-wide situation."

This is where your trips to the plant can really begin to pay off. Call the estimators, or perhaps the production planning people; there is always something you have to talk to them about.

Then find out:

1. Is the factory busy with orders they received before the price rise?

2. Are incoming orders holding up? ("How's the backlog, Ray? Still six weeks to production?")

If the answer to both of these questions is "Yes," you know that the price rise will soon be into your territory. Your plant just happened to be first this time.

But if the answer to the first question is "Yes" and the answer to the second is "No," there is usually one of two reasons:

1. The plant has been so busy they have decided to skim cream while they can. The treasurer has urged, "This is the time to get those extra-profit orders."

If this is the case, write to the sales manager. Point out that the factory is going to need GCE's business when things slow up, so they'd better be taken care of now! Some manufacturers can never see beyond a full three months' schedule.

2. Someone has been bidding for their hand in merger. New rates always look good when they are applied back-

wards. ("See how much more we're going to make this year . . . and on the same volume of business!")

In this case you had better point out that their real profit picture is going to look awful if they lose business the way they've been pricing quotes these last three months.

Price is the flimsiest reason of all for losing a key account. Make sure it isn't a cover-up for a much more important reason. Check the account thoroughly; you'll rarely find that price alone (unless, of course, you've been outrageous) is the reason a key account will drop you.

SHOULD YOU GO OVER A BUYER'S HEAD?

Not if you are losing out for business reasons: lower prices, bad deliveries, new materials which you have been unable to match, slipshod quality control, etc. If GCE keeps the buyer on the job, the Vice President—Purchasing must have confidence in the buying decisions that are being made. If that confidence is unjustified, economics will soon let everyone know about it and you'll be back in.

Don't go over a buyer's head to rest your claim on the vague quality of loyalty: "I've done a good job for GCE for seven years." They'll tell you they've paid your invoices promptly for seven years. And their first loyalty is to GCE, as yours is to your business.

Suppose you are successful. You'll find that going over a buyer's head may bring momentary revenge and satisfaction ("That'll show 'em"). It may even get you back in for a short while. But there it ends. The buyer—and everyone else in the plant—will always resent you and go out of their way to make sure some other supplier or agent looks better than you.

Moreover, the buyer will let every acquaintance in the industry know that you are the type who heads for someone higher "every time I place the business elsewhere." After a while buyers will head for the hills when they see you coming. You are a menace to their self-satisfaction and their jobs. Imagine what a reputation like that will do for your sales!

Above all, if you impugn a buyer's integrity, even if you are justified, the type of gratitude you get for doing it is never very long-lasting. No one likes or trusts the bearer of bad news— "That rep must have squealed because what's-his-name couldn't let anyone else in on it." And if you don't have conclusive proof but are just doing it out of frustration . . . it may cost you your whole business.

"I've got nothing to lose. They're not going to give me any more business anyway." If that is your basic reason for going over a buyer's head, you may just as well add, "And they never will."

Ninety-eight percent of the time, going over a buyer's head is wasted motion.

The other 2 percent of the time is tricky, too. Say you meet the president of the corporation at a golf course and you both hit it off. He gives you a note to his buyer. Make sure the buyer understands you didn't even know who the president was when you met him; that you don't do business that way; that if the buyer wishes, you won't even quote. You are merely calling here because the president told you to, and you don't want to get the buyer in trouble . . . and mean it when you say it.

The other one is where you have a family or social connection. Even then, don't lord it over the buyer. A smart buyer can see to it that your family connection sours in a short while with continual complaints of high prices, bad values—a million and one things. Production will be telling your connection, "Harvey (the buyer) told me we had to get it from so and so. I hear he's a relative of yours. But, Boss, his stuff is lousing up production and the rejects are out of this world!"

In both cases propitiate the buyer's hurt feelings (after all, he is a professional) at every opportunity. Try to make him see that your social or family connection may result in promotion for him.

PERSONAL ANTIPATHIES

You are going to lose a key account for personal reasons. The words "going to" are used because, in a case like this, you know all about it in advance if you are a rep with any experience at all.

There are certain people we annoy (and who annoy us—the feeling is usually mutual) just by existing. It has nothing to do with prejudice. It's just that our polarities are north and south and there's a whole world between us. We just can't stand one another.

Uninformed people always say business isn't done on personalities but on cold, hard facts. Anyone who has any experience at all knows that personality conflicts do exist and do tip the scales enormously.

This is the kind of case where the more you see the account, the more likely you are to lose it.

If you are a two- or three-man organization, you transfer the account immediately. You can always take it back when the buyer is transferred.

If you are a one-man outfit, or a salesrep whose company would listen to an explanation like that with disbelief, you have to figure out how you can neutralize this dislike:

1. You do as much as you can by mail and telephone.

2. When you are at the account's, you try and make more points than ever with the secretaries and, particularly, the production people who can specify your products.

You give superb service.

You smile like crazy and hide your feelings.

The buyer will never like you (or you the buyer), but at least it will save the account until the inevitable change comes and you get a buyer you can live with.

YOU MAY LOSE A KEY ACCOUNT IF THE PLANT DECIDES TO STOP PRODUCTION OF ONE ITEM

GCE, your key account, buys two items from you in tandem. The factory is thinking of stopping production of one of these items. You know very well that if GCE begins to buy one item from another plant, it will soon be buying both of them there . . . and you'll be out in the cold.

If GCE is large enough (and any key account should be), it is worth a trip to the factory. Point out that sales of ratchet heads depend on sales of ratchet holders—on which the factory does very well indeed.

Before they throw out production of ratchet heads, hadn't they better check around among all their sales reps and find out just how much they stand to lose if they stop the production of one item and keep on with the other?

You have to be a salesrep here, too. Remember that the treasurer has brought in those black-and-white figures. Point out that you are not trying to tell them how to run their business. At the same time let them know that without the GCEs of this world buying both items, the black-and-white figures are liable to turn red.

THOSE SMALL INTRAMURAL FIGHTS

It is surprising how fast small irritations can grow. Eliminate them quickly.

Your key account says they deserve a 2 percent discount. Your plant people are equally stubborn and say they don't. The buyer is becoming upset because he or she has been put into the middle of the whole thing—and has a lot of other things to worry about.

It's one of those small things that blow up into a big storm and can create a lot of trouble.

First get in touch with the sales manager . . . by telephone. Then write a strong note. It is up to the S M to intervene for you.

```
FROM:  You                          DATE......

TO:    J. R. Reagan, Sales Manager    RE: GCE

Dear J. R.:

This discount fight with GCE is blowing up
out of all proportion. I have to have some-
thing from you right away to show Paul
Andrews, the P.A., that we're on his side.
```

```
J. R., this tempest in a teapot is for the
birds. GCE mails out the check in ten days.
Our people say it should be on their desk in
ten days. It's a matter of two days one way
or the other. I don't have to tell you what
kind of account GCE is and how we've sweated
to build them up.

Please let me have that note clearing this up
today if possible.
```

The sales manager will show your note to the president, who will certainly cool off accounting.

Never pass by one of these small intramural fights because "they don't mean a damn thing." They are the little irritants which grow to be a big pain very quickly.

Selling is such an unhackneyed way of life no one can predict anything from day to day. That is why there were lots of questions in this book . . . and not all the answers. Most of the answers which will work for you can be provided only by you. But asking the right questions is just as important as—sometimes even more important than—the right answers. You know that from your sales training long ago, when you discovered that you had to ask the right questions in order to get the information you needed.

You still have to ask yourself the right questions in order to succeed in sales and in business.

Index